Passage to America

Queen Elizabeth I. By Nicholas Hilliard and Associates, from the initial letter of the charter authorizing the foundation of Emmanuel College, Cambridge, in 1584; by permission of the Master and Fellows, Emmanuel College, Cambridge.

Passage to America

Ralegh's Colonists Take Ship for Roanoke

by
Helen Hill Miller

Raleigh
America's Four Hundredth Anniversary Committee
North Carolina Department of Cultural Resources
1983

America's Four Hundredth Anniversary Committee

Lindsay C. Warren, Jr.
Chairman

Marc Basnight   Robert V. Owens, Jr.   Mrs. Margot Tillett
Andy Griffith   William S. Powell   Charles B. Wade, Jr.
Joseph W. Grimsley   L. Richardson Preyer   John F. Wilson IV
John P. Kennedy   David Stick   Charles B. Winberry, Jr.
                     Mrs. J. Emmett Winslow

John D. Neville, Jr.
Executive Director

Mrs. Marsden B. deRosset, Jr.
Assistant Director

Advisory Committee on Publications

William S. Powell
Chairman

Lindley S. Butler
Jerry C. Cashion
David Stick
Alan D. Watson

ISBN 0-86526-202-0

Contents

Maps and Illustrations vii

Foreword ix

A Note on Ralegh xi

Acknowledgments xiii

    I. The Setting 1

    II. The Ships 9

    III. The Art of Navigation 22

    IV. The Ship's Company 39

    V. Varied Cargo 56

    VI. The First Colony's Crossing 64

    VII. The Unreached Destination 74

Maps and Illustrations

Queen Elizabeth I . . . . Frontispiece
Sir Walter Ralegh 2
Durham House 3
Compton Castle 6
Plymouth Harbor 10
British Warship 12
Drawing by Shipbuilder Matthew Baker 13
Ship Designer and Assistant 13
Shipwright at Work 14
Flemish Warships 16,17
Ark Royal 19
Capture of Portuguese Carrack 20
Title Page of *The Arte of Navigation* (1596) 23
Frontispiece of *Light of Navigation* (1622) 25
John Dee 26
Gerardus Mercator and Jodocus Hondius 27
Title Page of *Regiment for the Sea* (1574) 28
Map from *Theatrum Orbis Terrarum* (1570) 29
Detail from Title Page of *A Prognostication Everlastinge* (1576) 31
Compass and Magnetized Fly Needle 33
Cross-Staff 34
Saint Christopher's Island 36
Atlantic Winds and Currents 37
Elizabethan Seaman 40
John Banester's Lecture on Anatomy 46
Sir John Hawkins 49
Sir Martin Frobisher 51
Capture of *Cacafuego* 53
Dartmouth Harbor 54
"Map of the World" (ca. 1550) 58
Sir Humphrey Gilbert 60
Sir Richard Grenville 65
Flagship *Tiger* 67
Fort at Mosquito Bay 68
Sir Thomas Cavendish 70
Map Showing Roanoke Island 71
Sir Francis Drake 75
Drake's Voyage of 1585-1586 77
Spain's Empire in the New World 79
Map of Portion of East Coast of North America 83

Foreword

America's Four Hundredth Anniversary Committee, formed in 1978 under the provisions of an act of the North Carolina General Assembly of 1973, was charged with recommending plans for the observance of the quadricentennial of the first English attempts to explore and settle North America. The committee has proposed to carry out a variety of programs to appeal to a broad range of people. Among these is a publications program that includes a series of booklets dealing with the history of the events and people of the 1580s.

Queen Elizabeth I of England enjoyed a reign that was for the most part peaceful. It was a period of prosperity, which saw the flourishing of a new interest in literature, religion, exploration, and business. English mariners began to venture farther from home, and in time talk began to be heard of hopes to establish naval bases and colonies in America. Men of the County of Devon in the southwest of England, seafarers for generations, played leading roles in this expansion. One of these, Walter Ralegh (as he most often wrote his name), became a favorite of the queen, and on him she bestowed a variety of honors and rewards. It was he to whom she granted a charter in 1584 authorizing the discovery and occupation of lands not already held by "any Christian Prince and . . . people." Ralegh promptly sent a reconaissance expedition to what is now North Carolina, and this was followed in due time by a colony under the leadership of Ralph Lane. Headquarters were established on Roanoke Island. After remaining for nearly a year and exploring far afield, Lane and his men returned to England in 1586.

In the summer of 1587 Governor John White and a colony of 115 men, women, and children arrived and occupied the houses and the fort left by Lane. The brief annals of this colony are recorded in a journal kept by the governor; they tell of certain problems that arose early—but they also record the birth of the first English child in America. The journal further explains why Governor White consented to return to England for supplies. His departure was the last contact with the settlers who constituted the "Lost Colony," renowned in history, literature, and folklore.

Although a casual acquaintance with the facts of these English efforts might suggest that they were failures, such was far from the case. Ralegh's expenditures of time, effort, and resources (in which he was joined by many others, including Queen Elizabeth herself) had salutary effects for England and certainly for all of present-day America. From Ralegh's initial investment in the reconaissance voyage, as well as from the colonies, came careful descriptions of the New World and samples of its products. The people of England, indeed of the Western world, learned about North America; because books were published based on what Ralegh's men discovered, they could soon read for themselves of the natives there and the promise of strange and wonderful new resources.

From these voyages and colonizing efforts came the conviction that an English nation could be established in America. In 1606, when another charter was about to be issued for further settlement, King James, who succeeded Queen Elizabeth at her death in 1603, called for advice from some of the men who had been associated with Ralegh. They assured the king that further efforts would surely succeed. With this the company was chartered, and it established England's first permanent settlement in America at Jamestown.

Because of Sir Walter Ralegh's vision, England persisted. Because of England's persistence and its refusal to yield to Spain's claims to the region, the United States today enjoys an English heritage. The English common law is the basis of American law; American legislative bodies are modeled on the House of Commons with the rights and freedoms that it developed over a long period of time; America's mother tongue is English, and it is the most commonly spoken language in the world—pilots and navigators on international airlines and the controllers who direct them at airports all over the world use English. Americans also share England's literary tradition: Chaucer, Beowulf, King Arthur, and Shakespeare are America's too, and Americans can enjoy Dickens and Tennyson, as well as Agatha Christie and Dorothy Sayers. America's religious freedom is in the English tradition as well, and several of this nation's Protestant denominations trace their earliest history to origins in England: the Episcopal church, certainly, but the Quakers, Baptists, Congregationalists, and Universalists as well.

America's Four Hundredth Anniversary Committee has planned many programs to direct national and even international attention to the significance of events that occurred from bases established by English men, women, and children, but notably Sir Walter Ralegh, in what is now North Carolina during the period 1584-1590. While some of the programs may be regarded as fleeting and soon forgotten, the publications are intended to serve as lasting reminders of America's indebtedness to England. Books and pamphlets covering a broad range of topics have been prepared by authors on both sides of the Atlantic. These, it is anticipated, will introduce a vast new audience to the facts of America's origins.

Lindsay C. Warren, Jr., *Chairman*
America's Four Hundredth Anniversary Committee

A Note on Ralegh

For the publications of America's Four Hundredth Anniversary Committee, it has been decided to use the spellings of certain surnames that were used by Elizabethan Englishmen themselves rather than modern versions of those names. Sir Walter Ralegh is not known to have used the spelling of his name that prevails today, although in his youth he did use a variety of other spellings. Every known signature of his from 1583 until his death in 1618 appears as *Ralegh*. The editors have also adopted the spelling of Harriot for Thomas Harriot (also spelled *Hariot*) and Fernandes for Simon Fernandes (also spelled *Fernández* and *Ferdinando*), although variant spellings may also be found. For further information on Ralegh, see T. N. Brushfield, "Sir W. Ralegh: A Plea for a Surname," in *Report and Transactions of the Devonshire Association*, XVIII (1886), 450-461.

Acknowledgments

My first gratitude is to O. B. Hardison, director of the Folger Shakespeare Library in Washington, D.C., and his colleagues, who opened to my use the unbelievable riches of its collections. Lady Stevens of East Worlington, Devon, arranged for me to enjoy a reader's privileges at the Devonian Association's headquarters in Exeter's Cathedral Close. On both sides of the Atlantic, the staffs of museums concerned with seafaring have been generous of their time.

The editor of the series of which this study of the Ralegh colonists' life at sea is a part, Professor William S. Powell of the University of North Carolina at Chapel Hill, arranged the assignment and has been the most supportive of counselors.

Lambert Davis, former director of the University of North Carolina Press, baptised the book, and his reading of the manuscript pointed the way to a number of improvements.

Those modern Hakluyts, David and Alison Quinn, and Professor Joyce Youings, Devon authority at the University of Exeter, have given me illuminating insights, and I am indebted to a number of others active in the preparations for the 400th anniversary celebrations.

I appreciate the skill of M. S. Raper of Elizabeth City, North Carolina, and Christopher Lehfeldt of Georgetown University in Washington, D.C., for coping with my indecipherable handwriting in successive typings of the text.

Helen Hill Miller

I. The Setting

Through the 1580s, Walter Ralegh's rise in the favor of his queen, Elizabeth I of England, astonished her court. His first appearance there was in December, 1581, when he arrived bearing military dispatches from Ireland. Within two years of that time, Elizabeth had established him in a style of living comparable to that maintained by the great aristocratic families of the realm. Seasoned courtiers, accustomed to finding rivals for the places and perquisites bestowable by their sovereign only among themselves, tossed their heads privately in disapproval of such largesse to an outsider.

Taller than most men, handsome of face and figure, elegant to extravagant in dress, thoroughly immersed in the new learning, a talented poet, Ralegh in his thirties was an ornament even to a court of Renaissance brilliance. John Aubrey, the seventeenth-century antiquarian who attended school with Ralegh's grand-nephews, remembered that "Q. Elizabeth loved to have all the servants of her court proper men, and, (as before said) Sr W. R.'s gracefull presence was no mean recommendation to him." The shrewd, witty, learned queen's long flirtation with the now-middle-aged Leicester had been abruptly interrupted in 1579 with her discovery of his secret marriage to her less-than-well-beloved relative, Lettice Knollys, the widowed Lady Essex. For a time, Leicester suffered disgrace and royal disfavor. Meanwhile, the queen saw to it that her new favorite, Ralegh, remained at her side, even commanding his presence at times when his attention veered toward maritime adventure.

Although her possessiveness turned him into a brightly feathered bird in a gilded cage, she was generous in her compensation: she installed Ralegh in magnificent apartments in Durham House, the ancient former palace of the bishops of Durham, in which her half-brother, King Edward VI, had granted her a life interest. Conveniently close to Whitehall, the establishment stood on the river side of the Strand, with grounds sloping down to the Thames. The stables were large enough to accommodate forty horses.

The queen initially supplied Ralegh with a sizable income by awarding him a monopoly on the sale of licenses to retail wines. At £1.0.0 per license (even though at first he subcontracted collections), Ralegh was assured of £700 a year. (By contrast, a ship captain's average annual salary was about £26.)

Within three years, the queen had granted her favorite a knighthood and a monopoly on the export of broadcloth, the latter worth about £3,500 per year in income. Wool had always been an English staple; in the early sixteenth century, increased supplies created by a widespread shift from subsistence agriculture to sheep pasturing had fostered the growth of domestic cloth manufacture.

Sir Walter Ralegh. Miniature (ca. 1584) by Nicholas Hilliard; National Portrait Gallery, London.

In 1585 Ralegh was appointed warden of the Stannaries (the organization that managed the weighing and stamping of the tin mined in his native West Country), lord lieutenant of Cornwall, and vice admiral of Cornwall and Devon. In 1586 and again in 1587 he was granted letters patent to colonize substantial areas in the counties of Cork and Waterford in Ireland, over 40,000 acres of which were reserved for his private use. In 1587, after discovering the Babington Plot against her life, Elizabeth gave Ralegh the confiscated estates of its perpetrator and named him her personal captain of the guard, a post that assured his constant presence, clad in silver armor. In 1585, when she denied him permission to lead his first colonists to the land that she allowed him to name Virginia in her honor, she bestowed upon him the resounding title Walter Ralegh Militis Domini et Gubernatoris Virginiae, a seal of office, and appointment as her master of horse.

Ralegh's meteoric ascent was not solely a personal triumph; it was an excep-

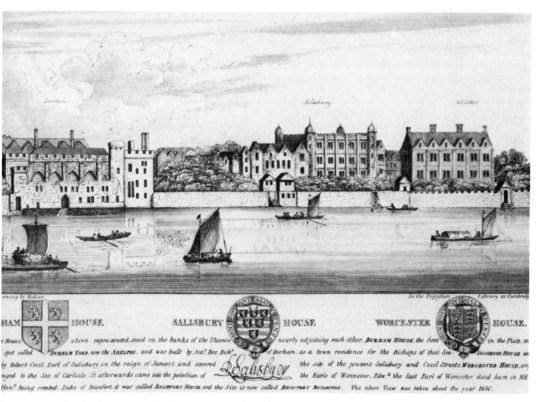

Elizabeth I granted to Walter Ralegh the use of spacious quarters at Durham House (left), the former London residence of the bishops of Durham on the Thames. From Robert Wilkinson, *London Illustrata* (London, 1819), plate 99; by permission of the Trustees of the British Museum, London.

tional illustration of a rapid and profound change in sixteenth-century English society. After Henry VIII took over the property of the church, a great deal of land suddenly came onto the market. Since feudal days, landholding had been the basis of gentility, and the laws of primogeniture and entail had assured the transfer of much of it intact from generation to generation. But in the mid-sixteenth century, the possibility of acquiring land enabled established families that had fallen on evil times to regain status. Thrifty farm tenants and town merchants, who prospered through increasing commerce, began to ascend the social and economic ladder. The size and composition of the gentry was changing.

Simultaneously, a change occurred in national outlook. The end of the Wars of the Roses had released England from its long preoccupation with domestic fratricide, and inhabitants of an island that had lain on the periphery of the medieval map began to look outward. English mariners had long plied between home ports and nearby Continental or even Mediterranean destinations, but by the sixteenth century, sailors who formerly had crept along coastlines were learning to venture out of sight of land.

Two other westward-facing powers, Spain and Portugal, had grasped the possibilities of their new position during the previous century. In 1438 the Portuguese prince, Henry the Navigator, gathered into his entourage men of nautical and geographic knowledge and later created a practical school of navigation at Lagos. Little by little, the prince stimulated his nation's seafarers to explore the Azores, the Canaries, the Cape Verdes, and the northern part of the West African coast. In 1497 another Portuguese, Vasco da Gama, rounded the Cape of Good Hope and sailed to India. This new sea route permitted resumption of the sale of Oriental goods to the West—interrupted when the rising Ottoman empire blocked the long-enjoyed monopoly of Venice and Genoa as middlemen for spices, silks, and pearls arriving in the eastern Mediterranean via overland camel routes. In 1492 the West Indies became part of the known world when Christopher Columbus, a native of Genoa, attempted a direct western voyage to China on behalf of Spain. A year later, Pope Alexander VI divided all newly discovered land between Spain and Portugal along a line of longitude running 100 leagues west of the Azores, a line modified by the two countries in 1494 to run 370 leagues west of the Cape Verde Islands. But by Elizabeth's time, England was moving to break up the Iberian monopoly.

Although no place in the British Isles is more than seventy miles from the sea, very few of the shires have as much seacoast as do Devon and Cornwall, which occupy the long peninsula that thrusts southwest and terminates in the Atlantic at Land's End. On both coasts of Devon, estuaries form convenient harbors. At the county's northwest corner, the Taw and the Torridge rivers combine to serve the towns of Barnstaple and Bideford. In the south in Ralegh's time, a long sequence of ports—Ottermouth, Exmouth, Dartmouth, Plymouth, Falmouth—opened to the sea.

Almost to a man, the greatest of the English captains who led their country into the contest for the New World were from this peninsula. The northwest section produced Richard Grenville and the brothers William and Stephen Borough. From the south came John and Richard Hawkins, Francis Drake, John Davis, Humphrey Gilbert, and Walter Ralegh. All were Devon men. Many of their families had lived in the county for centuries, but, with the exception of the Grenvilles, most of them came from relatively modest mid-sixteenth-century circumstances. Some of the captains descended from the gentry who undertook local public service as sheriffs and mayors, occasionally as members of Parliament, and still more occasionally as lords lieutenant and vice admirals. Others came from families that were wholly occupied in making a living.

The greatest span of social distance was that between Richard Grenville and Francis Drake. The Grenvilles had long occupied an imposing property at Stowe, just over the Devon-Cornwall county line below the port of Bideford; they had represented one or the other county in Parliament from at least 1388. During the sixteenth-century monastic sales, Grenville's grandfather acquired Buckland, formerly a Cistercian abbey north of Plymouth. In the mid-1550s Buckland became Richard's inheritance, his father Roger having gone down as master of the *Mary Rose*, second largest ship of the royal navy, in 1545.

By contrast, Drake's family lived in a tenant laborer's cottage at Crowndale, some six miles below Tavistock. The land, also acquired during the monastic sales, was leased by the Russell family to Drake's uncle. Drake's father, Edmund, sometimes listed as a shearman, sometimes as a sailor, was a religious reformer who approved the Church of England's new prayer book. When use of the book became obligatory in 1549, heartily disapproving Devon Catholics rose in armed revolt. The Drakes were among the conformists run out of the county during the violence. Because he was a relative of the Hawkinses (a Plymouth family that prospered as shipowners, shipbuilders, merchants, and privateers), Edmund Drake obtained a chaplaincy in the fleet. Taking orders, he was shortly installed as vicar at Upchurch, Kent, near the royal navy's marshaling station along the Medway River. There, in an old hulk of a ship stranded in the mud of the east shore, he reared a family that eventually numbered twelve sons. As soon as the eldest, Francis, was old enough to be apprenticed, he sailed with a captain in the coastal trade. In a few years young Drake inherited the captain's boat and, with the proceeds of its sale, returned to Plymouth and acquired his first trans-atlantic experience in the Hawkinses' West Indian ventures of the 1560s.

By blood or marriage, practically all of the great Devon sea captains were related. Two of the most famous were half brothers, children of Katherine Champernoune by successive husbands. Her first husband was Otho Gilbert of Compton Castle, an impressively fortified farm near Torquay; their sons were John, Humphrey, and Adrian. On Gilbert's death, she married Walter Ralegh, Sr., tenant of a farm near East Budleigh; their sons were Carew and Walter. It is an indication of the upward mobility of the times that four of her five sons—all except Adrian—became knights under Elizabeth.

Of the Devon confraternity, only the two half brothers, Gilbert and Ralegh, were university men. Humphrey Gilbert's Oxford college is not known. Walter Ralegh was a student at Oriel College in 1572, and only he became a courtier, eventually treading the perilous, jeweled path that ended for him, as for many others, at the block of the executioner.

A number of the new men had connections that acquired new dimensions over time. For example, the duties of the squirearchy could well have accounted for the willingness of young Francis Russell to stand godfather to the firstborn son of a tenant on his family's property. But Russell succeeded his father as earl of Bedford, and the baby grew up to be Sir Francis Drake, the first English circumnavigator.

Similarly, when Mistress Katherine Champernoune Ashley, great aunt of

Compton Castle, the home of the Gilbert family, dates from the fourteenth century and is shown here as it was sketched in the early nineteenth century. In 1930 Commander Walter Raleigh Gilbert brought it back into family ownership; during the ensuing years he and his wife Joan completed restoration of the structure and in 1951 placed it in the National Trust. From Rev. Daniel and Samuel Lysons, *Magna Brittania* (1822), VI, plate cccxlvi; by permission of the Folger Shakespeare Library.

Gilbert and Ralegh, was a member of the household of the forlorn Protestant Princess Elizabeth during the reign of her Catholic half sister Mary, the employment seemed of little account. But when Mistress Ashley continued in this service after the neglected princess became queen, she was able to divert Humphrey Gilbert from the Inns of Court into the royal presence. John Aubrey wrote that, because of the aunt's influence with Queen Elizabeth, nephew Gilbert

was for some time not only in the Queen's service, but in her favour, who would often confer with him in matters of learning, and in all probability about his favorite studies of Cosmography and Navigation, which could not but be favourable to his fortunes in the succeeding part of his life, and entitle him to such marks of his Sovereign's favour, as even his great merit would scarce have procured, if he had not been so early brought into her majesty's family.

Of the great captains, Grenville, Gilbert, and Ralegh all early foresaw that beyond exploring new continents and dislodging their first claimants, the building of an empire demanded colonization. Grenville and a number of West Country gentlemen made such a proposal in 1574. Gilbert attempted settlements in 1578 and 1583, and during 1584-1587 Ralegh achieved temporary success.

Political difficulties limited such ventures. In the eyes of the Portuguese and the Spanish, the pope's global division of the New World confirmed them alone as its possessors. England was obliged to contest their presence and at the same time to remain mindful of its interests in Europe. France was its hereditary enemy, and for some years England managed to pincer the French king's power by cooperation with Spain and its Low Country tributaries. This tie between England and Spain was reinforced when Henry VIII married the Spanish princess Catherine of Aragon. When their daughter Mary became queen, she married her Spanish cousin, Philip II. Until Mary's death in 1558, the throne of

England was shared by a prince who after 1556 also reigned as king of Spain. So in order to maintain amicable relations with Spain, Elizabeth carefully limited exploration and the taking of land in her name. When she issued letters patent to Grenville in 1574, to Gilbert in 1578, and to Ralegh in 1584, she authorized them only "to discover, finde, search out and view such remote, heathen and barbarous lands, countreys and territories, not actually possessed of any Christian prince or people."

Such a limitation did not hinder England's efforts to find a direct passage to the Orient—either to the northeast, above Europe, or to the northwest, above America. But problems with Spain did arise over settlement. When Gilbert found the climate of Newfoundland too severe to permit colonization, Ralegh launched a venture to settle the mid-Atlantic coast. The Spanish interpreted this attempt at English colonization as an act of deliberate trespass.

After 1580, English foreign policy had to adapt to a sudden shift in European power. King Sebastian of Portugal was unexpectedly killed in a battle with the Moors in Africa and left no direct heir. Philip II took advantage of the ensuing factional contests to absorb Portugal and its territorial claims into his kingdom. If left uncontested, this act would give Spain control of Portugal's west-facing coast, its Atlantic islands (the Azores, Madeira, the Canaries, and the Cape Verdes), and the Portuguese outposts along the Spice Island sea route from India to Canton. England could not afford to accept this major addition to Spanish holdings and thereby permit an increase in Spain's power and influence. Consequently, over the next eight years England and Spain were locked in an undeclared war that culminated in Philip's unsuccessful attempt to conquer England in 1588.

During this interval—the period during which Ralegh's colonizing ventures sailed—Elizabeth loaned ships and money for, and received major dividends from, voyages that the Spanish held to be pure piracy. The ever-cautious queen protected herself, however, by disowning as individual privateering the acts of sea captains who plundered Spanish ports and captured Spanish treasure fleets.

The extraordinary detail in which the voyages of this period are known can be attributed to two men, both named Richard Hakluyt. The elder was a member of the Middle Temple, England's ranking legal establishment. He inspired and aided his nephew, Ralegh's contemporary, who styled himself "Preacher and sometime student of Christ Church in Oxford," to compile an amazingly complete collection of firsthand accounts of the great English ventures.

In 1582 the younger Richard Hakluyt published a preliminary set of *Divers Voyages Touching the Discoverie of America,* and in 1589 he produced *Principall Navigations, Voyages, Traffiques and Discoveries of the English Nation.* This major work was further expanded in the years 1598-1600 to a length of 1¾ million words. The new editions added an assemblage of captains' logs, official and private correspondence, depositions by seamen, descriptions of places and peoples, and accounts of engagements fought on land and sea.

The Hakluyt collections reveal the meticulous observations of a number of sixteenth-century scientists—engaged by sponsors of the English voyages—

about a part of the Western Hemisphere previously unexamined. Among these scientific observers was Thomas Harriot, who wrote *A Briefe and True Report of the New Found Land of Virginia* after he and John White (his eventual illustrator) had lived a year with Ralegh's first colony.

About the same time that Harriot was preparing his manuscript, a Flemish engraver and publisher, Theodore de Bry, visited London and met the author and Hakluyt. Then, or perhaps subsequently, de Bry examined John White's watercolors. Some years later at his press in Frankfurt, he made woodcuts from the White watercolors to illustrate a new edition of Harriot's *Briefe and True Report*, which was published in 1590. Then, in collaboration with Hakluyt, he began a twenty-five-part, illustrated *Collectiones peregrinationum in Indiam orientalem et Indiam occidentalem*, which he, and after his death his sons, published from 1590 to 1634. It appeared not only in Latin but also in a variety of European languages.

This was the setting in which Richard Grenville, Humphrey Gilbert, and Walter Ralegh applied to the queen to establish permanent English footholds in America and attracted colonists to venture their futures on the passage to the newfound lands.

II. The Ships

When the prospective planters of Walter Ralegh's initial expedition, gathering for departure in 1585, looked down from the high esplanade of the Hoe across the ample roadstead of Plymouth Harbor, the little ships that were to take them across 3,000 miles of open ocean were not readily distinguishable from other vessels moored alongside—vessels whose destinations were no farther away than the trading centers of nearby Continental coasts.

Some of the prospective colonists had doubtless seen great ships at anchor offshore over the years—the 1,000-ton *Henry Grace à Dieu (Great Harry)*, which in 1520 had borne Henry VIII in effulgent display across the Channel to meet King Francis I of France at the Field of the Cloth of Gold; the 1,000-ton *Triumph*, largest of Queen Elizabeth's fleet; and the 700-ton *Jesus of Lubeck*, bought by Henry from Hanseatic merchants, inherited by Elizabeth, leased by her to John Hawkins for his second and third slaving voyages to the West Indies, and lost when a Spanish fleet defeated him at San Juan de Ullua in the Gulf of Mexico in 1568.

Over the years, even private fleets included some major ships. In 1583 Ralegh acquired the 260-ton *Bark Ralegh*, intending to command her on Sir Humphrey Gilbert's second colonial effort—only to have the queen forbid him to leave her court. In 1587 Elizabeth purchased his *Ark Ralegh* while it was still under construction; renamed the *Ark Royal*, the 800-ton vessel sailed as the flagship aboard which her lord high admiral, Lord Howard of Effingham, led the attack against the Spanish Armada the following year.

The Virginia-bound planters may likewise have seen some of the great prizes taken by English privateers: broad-beamed Portuguese carracks that had rounded the Cape of Good Hope with spices and silks from the Orient, or high-pooped Spanish caravels weighted with gold and silver of the conquered Incas of Peru. These captured vessels were brought home for their spoils to be divided among the queen, her courtiers and investors, the victuallers of the expeditions, and the officers and crews.

But the excitement of such great spectacles was a rarity: the tonnage of the ships on which Ralegh's colonists traveled ranged upward from 20 to 30 for some of their pinnaces to an exceptional maximum of 250 for their largest ships. Most ships weighed from 90 to 160 tons. (Tonnages were calculated according to the builder's estimate of a ship's capacity to carry 252-gallon tuns [hogsheads] of wine.) Their keelsons ran about 60 feet, their overall length about 100 feet, their maximum breadth of main deck at the waist, 35 feet. Sir Francis Drake's 160-ton *Golden Hind* was just over 70 feet long, 24 feet wide, and 12 feet deep.

Plymouth Harbor, from which Sir Walter Ralegh's expeditions to the New World departed. From a mid-sixteenth-century manuscript, Cotton Augustus, I, 1, f. 41; courtesy of the Trustees of the British Library, London.

10

No precise specifications for an actual vessel of the Tudor period are known to exist: representations of particular ships and of shipping in general must be based on woodcuts and oil paintings of the time, although records of construction and performance contain partial details. Despite this lack of specific information, it appears that over the period of the Ralegh voyages, shipbuilding improved considerably. The appointment of the knowledgeable Sir John Hawkins as Queen Elizabeth's navy treasurer in 1578 hastened the adoption of a number of structural changes. Because of these changes as well as a difference in overall size, English ships of the latter sixteenth century differed radically from those of Portugal and Spain.

A ship weighted at bow and stern with top-heavy superstructures as in the Spanish and Portuguese designs was certain to pitch; after a few years of sailing, the leverage of the weight at both ends caused the ship to become "hogged" in the middle. Portuguese shipbuilders enlarged cargo space by increasing the beam (width) of their vessels to about half their length. Having to wait for the semiannual monsoons in the Indian Ocean, Portuguese shipping could not accomplish the long route around the Cape of Good Hope in less than a year. Consequently, large cargo capacity was important. Spanish shipwrights likewise stressed size as a pertinent factor in treasure ships, which required an entire season to make the round trip from Spain to the Gulf of Mexico. Spanish galleons, essentially freighters, were usually accompanied on their way home by armed escorts.

Lacking the sources of rich cargoes enjoyed by their rivals and predecessors in open ocean navigation, the English built ships that were small and "race-built." English captains preferred craft that were longer and leaner, with length and breadth in a ratio closer to three-to-one—and by the time of the Armada four-to-one. After Matthew Baker, the queen's chief shipwright, proposed a model that compared the shape of a good ship to that of a fish, English superstructures were markedly reduced in size; the change lessened topheaviness, added speed, and increased maneuverability. After the mid-sixteenth century, the siding of the newer ships was carvel-built, with the boards abutting each other instead of overlapping, as on the older, clinker-built vessels. The new ones leaked less.

Three masts—a foremast, a mainmast, and a mizzenmast—were standard, and frequently a bonaventure (a fourth mast) was added at the stern. More and more ships were fore-and-aft rigged, with canvas varying according to location. On these, in addition to a spritsail at the bow, square sails were carried on fore- and mainmasts, often with topsails above and attachable bonnets and drabblers to lengthen them. By contrast, lateen sails that could be swung to one side of the boat or the other were routinely used on mizzen and bonaventure masts. One Fletcher of Rye had discovered that the flexibility of these swinging sails enabled ships thus equipped to be sailed closer to the wind than conventional square-rigged vessels.

The holds contained one or two closed decks, usually with only a 3-foot clearance between them. Originally, cooking was done in a sandpit placed for steadiness at the bottom of the hold; but as time went on, the cook room, with a brick platform, was placed in the forecastle (the fire was extinguished in rough weather). Midship steadiness was reserved for the surgeon (if one was aboard), who customarily occupied a small bottom-deck space, where he undertook operations and sewed up wounds.

Covering the holds was the orlop, a deck that ran the entire length of the ship and was exposed at the waist. Forward, behind the bowsprit, this deck was

A British warship of the sixteenth century, with the Tudor rose and the letters *ER* for Elizabeth Regina. From MS Rawl. A. 192; Bodleian Library, Oxford.

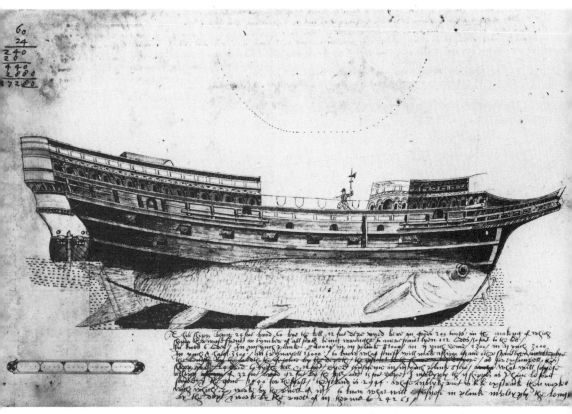

At the time of the first British colonization in America, ship design was changing. Shipbuilder Matthew Baker compared the shape of a good ship with that of a fish. From Pepysian Library MS 2820; by permission of the Master and Fellows, Magdalene College, Cambridge.

A sixteenth-century ship designer and his assistant. Pepysian Library, MS 2820.

topped by the forecastle, which often consisted of two decks, and at the stern by the sterncastle, where, aft of the mainmast, a quarterdeck supported at least one, and more often two, poop decks. One of these usually had a gallery across the stern, from which the captain-general (a ship's commanding officer) could observe the sea around him.

The helmsman controlled the ship's rudder by a tiller that was moved from side to side by a whipstaff from the deck above. Crewmen raised and lowered the anchor by turning a spoked capstan normally located forward of the mainmast.

The kind and position of guns carried by ships of different sizes varied accord-

A cross section of a hull under construction with a shipwright at work. Pepysian Library, MS 2820.

ing to each vessel's design and date of construction. On earlier ships, light artillery was stationed along the open deck to riddle enemy sails and rigging (yardarms were often tipped with knives to serve the same purpose) and to fire on attackers as they moved in to grapple and swarm aboard. Heavy netting was strung above the open deck to protect defending soldiers and seamen from falling rigging and to make it more difficult for attackers to clamber over the sides. Once a ship was boarded, the engagement, except for occurring in a cramped space, differed little from battle on land. Fighting was hand to hand at close quarters.

Later, as new naval strategies and much heavier guns were developed, long-range cannon were placed below decks. When the *Ark Royal* was armed to face the Armada, she carried 4 sixty-pounders, 4 thirty-pounders, 12 eighteen-pounders, 12 nine-pounders, and 6 six-pounders as well as smaller guns. The big guns were movable; during normal sailing, the openings through which their muzzles protruded in battle were tightly covered to keep out the sea. But when the gunports were open during engagements, even a sudden change of wind could pour water into the hold. The *Mary Rose* filled and sank when she keeled over in an unexpected breeze off Portsmouth during an attempted French invasion in 1545. After advances in gunnery made it possible for broadsides of heavy cannonballs, fired from a distance, to sink an enemy ship by penetrating her hull or immobilize an adversary by dismasting her, naval tactics and strategy became an independent branch of military science.

At shallow-water ports or during exploration of sites on harborless shores, each ship required at least one pinnace and several longboats for use by landing parties. Longboats were usually secured on the main deck amidships. Pinnaces, some of which were of very fair size, often sailed on their own; small ones, if carried, were knocked down for assembly at destination. Ships normally brought tools and supplies of metal so that new boats could be built at stops where wood was available.

Except during marauding expeditions, English ships identified their nationality by displaying the flag of St. George, a red cross on a white field. Many Tudor illustrations show additional flags—a jack on the bowsprit, an ensign at the stern, and one or more streamers at the mast tops. The royal standard was raised when the sovereign was aboard or if the lord high admiral was present. By Elizabeth's time, the royal ships of the line had been divided into three squadrons—van, center, and rear. Thereafter, the lord high admiral, as the representative of his sovereign, flew the royal standard at the main and a St. George at the fore; each vessel in his squadron flew a flag of St. George at the main. The admiral of the van flew St. Georges at the main and fore, and each ship in his squadron flew a St. George at the fore. The admiral of the rear (often called the wing) squadron flew St. Georges at the main and mizzen (and bonaventure, if there was one), and each ship in his squadron flew a St. George at the mizzen (and bonaventure, if any).

When a fleet was moving in concert, it signaled with flags and sails by day or with lanterns by night in an attempt to keep members together. The orders for

The sixteenth-century change in the arming of warships is shown by two works of the Flemist artist Pieter Breughel the Elder. In the earlier years of the century, guns were located only on the open deck, as shown above in the engraving *Nef de bande ou de Haut bord* (B 23,124).

Later, long-range cannons were placed below decks, as pictured by the etching and engraving *Ship of the Line* (B 18,786). From the Rosenwald Collection, National Gallery of Art, Washington.

17

Sir Humphrey Gilbert's 1583 voyage listed among his responsibilities as admiral his duty to guide the fleet by flying his flag by day and displaying a lantern on the mainmast by night. (Because of the fire hazard, the only lights permitted on board after dark were the signal lantern and a binnacle light, which allowed the helmsman to keep and record his course.) By day, signals were given by hoisting and striking topsails in agreed order. By night, if the admiral decided to shorten sail, he showed two lights until answered by all other ships, each showing one. If he made more sail, he displayed three lights, one above the other. If he hulled down, he waved a light on a pole over his regular light. In case of prolonged fog, he fired two shots each evening, and the other ships were to answer with one. If a ship started to leak or developed other difficulties, its captain fired a shot and hung a light as a signal for others to approach; they acknowledged by showing one light briefly. Every evening, each ship hailed the admiral and those ahead fell astern of him; in coastal waters, this was done both morning and evening. If the admiral desired a conference of the fleet, he showed his ensign, normally flown at the stern, in the main shrouds.

For one all-too-frequent contingency, only frail means existed to keep a fleet together. Whether in the vicious storms of the Bay of Biscay or in the hurricanes of the Caribbean, the risk of violent separation was ever present. Prior to sailing, or during conferences at sea, fleet commanders designated ports at which scattered ships would attempt to reassemble. Sealed orders, to be destroyed in case of capture, contained watchwords to permit recognition in the dark.

Separations occurred during almost every voyage. Sometimes they ended in unexpected and welcome reunions of ships feared to have been lost. Sometimes captains abandoned an expedition and headed for home. In the latter case, the admiral of the fleet might approve, or at least accept, such a departure if damage to a ship or sickness among a crew seemed to him to justify a captain's decision. He might, however, condemn a captain's action as cowardice, desertion, or mutiny. But an admiral could do little to prevent it or to punish a captain prior to their return to England.

Ralegh's close association with ships ranged from his own 800-ton *Ark Ralegh*, 140-ton *Roebuck*, and 50-ton *Dorothie* to the fleets with which he served in expeditions from Cadiz to Guiana. Some thirty years after the Roanoke voyages, he set down his views on how a ship could best be built and fitted out. He was then a prisoner in the Tower of London by command of James I but at the same time a companion and confidant of the king's heir-apparent, young Henry, Prince of Wales. Sir Walter dedicated his *Observations Concerning the Royal Navy and Sea Service* to Henry, whose death at eighteen in 1612 left Ralegh to the mercies of James.

The English navy was then suffering serious neglect. The Spanish menace had ended, and the great English sea captains were gone. Ralegh questioned the quality of their successors, who frequently had been chosen "by the mediation of great men for the preferment of their servants" and "now and then by virtue of the purse." Naval leadership, he asserted, should be drawn from men with the most experience in sea service and those who possessed "judgment and practice in the utensils and necessaries belonging to equipping, even from the batt's end to the very keelson of a ship."

Ralegh, who favored smaller ships, regarded a length of 100 feet and a breadth of 35 feet as a good size. He pointed out that "a ship of six hundred tons will carry as good ordnance as a ship of twelve hundred tons; and though the greater have double her number, the lesser will turn her broadsides twice before the greater can wind once." His six principal requirements for a warship were that she be strong, swift, and stout-sided and that she carry her guns out in all weather, hull and try well, and stay well when boarding and turning on a wind were required.

Sheathing of all navy ships, Ralegh observed, would forestall the expensive necessity of caulking and repairing the vessels on nearly an annual basis. As to quarters, he insisted: "Man may not expect the ease of many cabins and safety at once in sea-service. Two decks and a half is sufficient to yield shelter and lodging

The *Ark Royal* was the English flagship in the fight against the Spanish Armada in 1588. In the previous year, it had been commissioned by Sir Walter Ralegh as the *Ark Ralegh*; Queen Elizabeth bought it from him and renamed it while it was still on the stocks. From an engraving by C. J. Visscher; by permission of the Trustees of the British Museum.

19

for men and mariners, and no more charging at all higher, but only one low cabin for the master."

Aware that a navy, like an army, travels on its stomach, Ralegh castigated the all-too-frequent bad victualing of the service and claimed that it led "to the great slander of the navy, to the discouragement of all them that are pressed thereunto, and to the hinderance of his majesty's service." One of his complaints was that suppliers, to save money, often delivered beer in old barrels that had been used for other purposes,

stale cask that hath been used for herrings, train-oil, fish, and other such unsavory things, and thereinto fill the beer that is provided for the king's ships. Besides, the cask is commonly so ill-hooped, as that there is waste and leaking made of the fourth part of all the drink.

Ralegh thought the recent change in the structure of merchant ships that had resulted in the galley being placed in the forecastle instead of at the bottom of the hull should be imitated in warships. The danger of fire, as well as the diffusion of heat, smoke, and smells in the cargo area, would thus be reduced. Furthermore,

if any storms arise, or the sea grow so high as that the kettle cannot boil in the forecastles, yet having with their beer and biscuit, butter and cheese, and with their pickled herrings, oil, vinegar, and onions, or with their red herrings and dry sprats, oil and mustard, and other like provisions that needs no fire, these supply and varieties of victuals will very sufficiently content (and nourish) men for a time, until the storm be overblown that kept the kettle from boiling.

The Spanish and Portuguese built large vessels such as the Portuguese carrack (above, center) to transport rich cargoes from their colonies. The English and Dutch vessels, surrounding and capturing the carrack, were smaller ships built by countries which at that time lacked such sources of wealth. From *Het Journal van Joris van Speilbergen, Delft* (1605); courtesy of the Library of Congress, Rare Book Room.

Remembering earlier days, Ralegh closed his remarks by responding to a question often asked since the defeat of the Armada:

why should his majesty and the state be troubled with this needless charge of keeping and maintaining so great a navy in such exquisite perfection and readiness, the times being now peacable..., as well by the uniting of the two nations [the crowns of Scotland and England became one when James VI of Scotland suceeded Elizabeth in 1603 as James I of England], as by the peace which we hold with Spain, and all other Christian princes?

His answer was:

we must not flatter and deceive ourselves, to think that this calm and concord proceeds either from a settled immutable tranquility in the world, (which is full of alterations and various humours,) or from the good affections of our late enemies, who have tasted too many disgraces, repulses, and losses, by our forces and shipping, to wish our state so much felicity as a happy and peaceable government, if otherwise they had power to hinder it: and therefore though the sword be put into the sheath, we must not suffer it there to rust, or stick so fast, as that we shall not be able to draw it readily, when need requires.

III. The Art of Navigation

If the ships in which the colonists sailed were like the craft employed in the coastal trade near home, the demands upon their captains were very different: transatlantic navigation, the piloting of a vessel out of sight of land for days or weeks, required far more skill and far more ability to use instruments than did the navigation of coastal waters. By the time the old island-hopping course via the Faeroes and Iceland was replaced by a more direct crossing to Newfoundland, sea captains and their crews had acquired much open-ocean experience, and some of the knowledge necessary to make more accurate calculations for Atlantic crossings was in the process of development.

A time gap, however, existed between development of the knowledge and its dissemination. On the Continent, the Renaissance impulse to understand the physical world had in recent decades pushed aside geographic assumptions unrevised since the time of the Greek philosophers and replaced them with actual findings. Cosmology and global geography became active intellectual pursuits. But the interest of the scientists probing the world's physical secrets was in pure, rather than applied, knowledge. Most of these learned men knew each other, and they overcame difficulties of communication in their respective languages by speaking and writing in Latin—even using Latin translations or versions of their given names. In their intimate circle, a decade or more could elapse between the development of a hypothesis and its appearance in print. Meanwhile, they circulated the new idea among themselves in manuscript.

Yet, as Spain and Portugal undertook their astounding voyages, the pertinence of the new knowledge to the art of navigation began to bring theory and practice together. To fill out new global maps, scientists needed navigators' sketches of coasts they had explored; and ocean-crossing mariners needed scientists' calculations. Henry the Navigator had first brought these interests together. Before long, the rulers of Spain as well as Portugal appointed chief pilots to oversee the instruction of others. In Seville, Spain's Casa de Contratación was not only an overseas trade center but also a navigational training school, setting formal examinations for pilots. In England, Henry VIII, "with princely liberalities erected three guilds or brotherhoods"—the Trinity Houses at Deptford, Kingston, and Newcastle. In 1546 he gave his navy an administrative structure by setting up the Navy Board at Deptford.

Various texts on the art of navigation, some of them in simplified question-and-answer form, began to be published in English. Knowledge of navigation also spread by movement of persons. Columbus was by no means the only pilot who went from country to country in search of royal patronage: the Venetian Caboto became John Cabot, a trader in Bristol, and his son Sebastian served

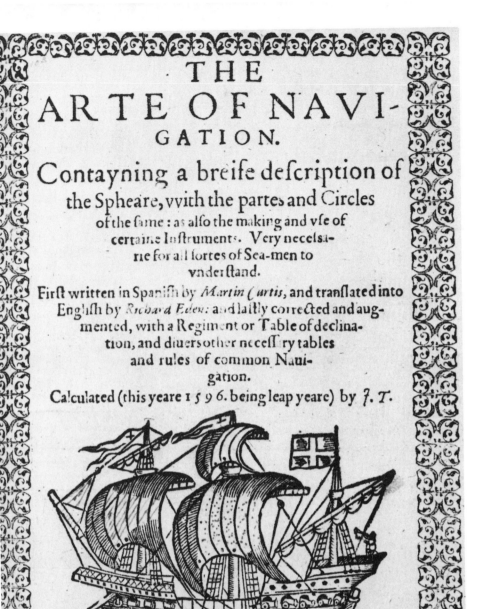

THE ARTE OF NAVI-
GATION.

Contayning a breife defcription of
the Spheare, vvith the partes and Circles
of the fame : as alfo the making and vfe of
certaine Inftruments. Very necefsa-
rie for all fortes of Sea-men to
vnderftand.

Firft written in Spanifh by *Martin Curtis*, and tranflated into
Englifh by *Richard Eden*: and laftly corrected and augmented, with a Regiment or Table of declination, and diuers other necefsary tables
and rules of common Naui-
gation.

Calculated (this yeare 1 5 9 6. being leap yeare) by *I. T.*

Imprinted at London by *Edw. Allde* for *Hugh Aftley*, by the
afsignes of *Richard Watkins*, and are to be folde at
Sainct Magnus corner. 1 5 9 6.

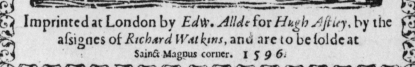

Essential equipment for sixteenth-century English ship captains included the
seaman's manual *The Arte of Navigation*, first translated into English in 1561 by Richard
Eden from Martin Cortés's *Arte de Navegar*. Title page from a 1596 edition by permission of the Folger Shakespeare Library.

during one period as pilot major to Emperor Charles V of Spain and on another occasion as grand pilot to Edward VI of England.

Some of the newly applied science came to England through the considerable English merchant colony located in Seville, Spain, and its river-mouth port, San Lucár. Stephen Borough, who was familiar with the Spanish examinations for pilots, persuaded Cambridge scholar Richard Eden to translate Martin Cortés's *Arte de Navegar* into English. Published in 1561, it remained in active use until superseded by John Davis's *Seamans Secrets* in 1595. Eden, who had already translated the Milanese historian Peter Martyr's *Decades of the Newe Worlde, or West India*, underscored the fact that in addition to lands preempted by the Spaniards, "there yet remaineth another portion of that mainland reaching toward the Northeast"—territory as yet uninhabited by Christians and perhaps containing a northwest passage to the Orient.

Yet, difficulties attended the transfer of learning to action. Very few English ship captains knew Latin, and little of the knowledge contained in the Latin texts was adapted to their needs. Those who were veterans of many voyages, moreover, were apt to sniff with suspicion at treatises by scientists whose familiarity with water transport, they sneered, might be confined to the wherries that plied the Thames.

In Portugal, Diogo do Conto wrote:

> I am not any friend at all of these tap-room pilots, these men with their great mappemondes who always carry their spheres with them, these men who from always looking at the sun and the moon and the stars and the heavens while they are sailing run the ship aground. . . . I am very much a friend of sea-going pilots, who go from pages to cabinboys and from cabinboys to sailors, and from there they push their way upward until they become mate or pilot, because the experience of these men is a living knowledge, not a painted one, of the land, of the sea, of the birds, of the sea weed, of the seals, of the Cape of Good Hope, and of the depths where they throw their lead, of the parts of the sea that are charted, and of the coast; even the fish that follow the ship they catch for information about their voyage, and about the latitude where they are.

As early as about 1520, Sir Thomas More's brother-in-law John Rastell, in his *New Interlude and a merry on the Nature of the Four Elements*, had called for more presentation of pertinent information in the vernacular:

> . . . divers pregnant wits be in this land
> As well of noblemen as of mean estate
> Which nothing but English can understand.
> Then if cunning Latin books were translate
> Into English, well correct and approbate,
> All subtle science in English might be learned.

At the end of the century, William Barlow's manual, *The Navigators Supply*, was still urging consultation between pilots and "Students of the Mathematikes."

By the time of the Roanoke voyages, various highly placed and learned Englishmen had traveled on the Continent and met ranking scientists there; at home, intellectual courtiers studied the science of oceanic navigation. About 1582 Ralegh engaged an Oxford mathematician and astronomer, Thomas Harriot, to join his entourage at Durham House as his mathematical tutor, and

Although sometimes contemptuous of each other, theory-minded scientists and practical-minded sea captains shared knowledge concerning ocean navigation. In the frontispiece of W. Z. Blaeu's *Light of Navigation* (1622), they confer, flanked by symbolic figures related to seafaring. By permission of the Folger Shakespeare Library.

for the next decade Harriot held seminars on navigation there. In dedicating to Ralegh the Latin edition of Peter Martyr's *De Orbe Novo*, which he published in 1587, Richard Hakluyt praised the results:

Ever since you perceived that skill in the navigator's art, the chief ornament of an island kingdom, might attain its splendour amongst us if the aid of the mathematical sciences were enlisted, you have maintained in your household Thomas Hariot, a man pre-eminent in those studies, at a most liberal salary, in order that by his aid you might acquire those noble sciences in your leisure hours, and that your own sea-captains, of whom there are not a few, might link theory with practice, not without almost incredible results.

Among the learned men who joined in this endeavor, Cambridge mathematician and astronomer John Dee was probably the greatest contributor. Part scientist and part Welsh necromancer, he traveled the Continent collecting nautical instruments and books for his library at Mortlake near Kew. In Brussels he met Gerard Mercator, whose *Mappamonde* was just out, and he lectured on Euclid in Paris. In 1570, in a preface to Henry Billingsley's translation of Euclid,

English mathematician and astronomer John Dee, a foremost contributor among learned men who developed new science for sixteenth-century ocean navigation. By permission of the Trustees of the British Museum.

Dee defined the new needs of a master pilot:

What nede, the *Master Pilote*, hath of other Artes, here before recited, it is easie to know; as of *Hydrographie, Astronomie, Astrologie,* and *Horometrie*. Pre-supposing continually, the common Base, and foundacion of all: namely, *Arithmeticke* and *Geometrie*.

Acquainted with Dee, but far closer than he to the practicing mariner, was William Bourne, trained gunner, "capital inhabitant," and sometime mayor of Gravesend on the Thames in the heart of the shipping district. Bourne was a scholar, though where he learned languages is unknown: his works suggest that he was familiar with modern European languages as well as Latin, and he clearly had access to, but did not own, an extensive library. His concern was to provide the sailors he knew and saw daily with a manual containing information of practical and immediate use to them. His *Regiment for the Sea* (1574) went far toward accomplishing that purpose.

Gerardus Mercator (left), renowned Renaissance geographer, and Jodocus Hondius, engraver and illustrator of sixteenth-century voyages, with their world globes. From the first edition in English of Mercator's *Atlas*, Amsterdam, 1636; courtesy of the Library of Congress.

Beginning with Bourne, the writing of such practical manuals became popular. In Holland in 1584 Lucas Waghenaer, a retired seaman, published his *Spieghel der Zeevaert*. Four years later Sir Christopher Hatton, Queen Elizabeth's vice-chamberlain, had Waghenaer's book printed in English as *The Mariners Mirrour*, with new charts made in London. By mid-century, skilled London tool-makers were marketing the navigational instruments recommended by the new authorities. Although Bourne instructed his readers on how to make their own apparatus, most of the superb equipment used by the Yorkshire explorer Martin Frobisher during his 1576 voyage in search of a northwest passage came from the London workshop of Humfrey Cole, a ranking instrument maker.

¶A REGIMENT
for the Sea:
Conteyning moſt profitable Rules,
Mathematical experiences, and perfeᵉt
knovvledge of Nauigation, for all Coaſtes and
Countreys: moſt needefull and neceſſarie for all Seafaring
men and Trauellers, as Pilotes, Mariners,
Marchants.ꝛc. Exactly deuiſed and
made by VViiliam
Bourne.

A Sea
aſtorolob
or ring.

¶ Imprinted at London by Thomas Hacket, and
are to be ſolde at his ſhop in the Royall Exchaunge,
at the Signe of the Greene Dragon.

William Bourne's *Regiment for the Sea* (1574) provided sailors with one of the best practical manuals of navigation. A picture of an astrolabe appears on the title page of this first edition. Courtesy of the Library of Congress, Rare Book Room.

During the period in which Ralegh's colonists went to sea, captains in charge of transatlantic voyages were likely to have on board most of the navigational instruments recommended by the new manuals. The aid these instruments afforded and the limitations their inaccuracies imposed give insight into the state of the art in the latter decades of the sixteenth century.

Among the most essential were the maps and charts zealously guarded in the

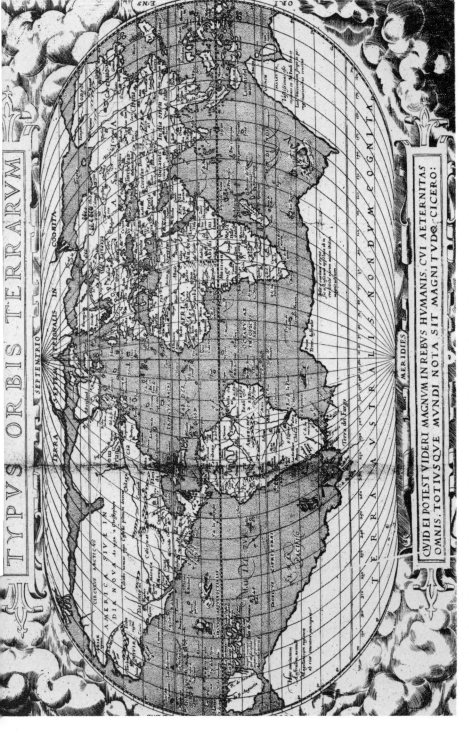

A world map from Abraham Ortelius's *Theatrum Orbis Terrarum* (1570) displays in detail oceans and continents that previous maps had indicated only vaguely. From Richard Hakluyt, *Principall Navigations* (1589), foldout map facing sig. A1.; by permission of the Folger Shakespeare Library.

captains' cabins and sure to be seized by captors if opportunity presented itself. The earliest of these documents were frequently laid out on whole sheepskins, with the neck to the left to indicate west; later, most were on parchment. The speed with which the contents of maps changed was an indication of the rapid increases in precise knowledge of lands that had been labeled terra incognita only a few years before. Instead of Ptolemy's Mediterranean-centered world with nothing to the west, an ill-drawn and sketchy Orient to the east, and a formless Africa below, Ortelius's *Typus Orbis Terrarum* displayed a global array of continents and oceans with vagueness confined largely to the regions around the poles.

Yet, though their geographic outlines improved, the new charts continued to present inaccuracies. The maps displayed parallel, equidistant, and horizontal circles of latitude north and south of the equator. These circles were usually intersected at right angles by lines of longitude that were vertical, equidistant, and parallel. The lines of latitude were correct and very useful, but the lines of longitude were in fact by no means parallel; they converged to a point at each pole and intersected the circles of latitude at right angles only at the equator. This important mistake was recognized and given first place among "Errors in the Arte of Navigation commonly practised" in A *Prognostication everlastinge*... *published by Leonard Digges Gentleman. Lately corrected and augmented by Thomas Digges, his sonne.* and sold in London in 1576.

Mercator's chart of 1569 did not commit this error, but an instrument capable of truly accurate calculation of longitude at sea was not available before the eighteenth century. (Until Charles II founded Greenwich Observatory in 1675, the zero [prime] line of longitude was laid in the Atlantic Ocean running through Ferro in the Canaries.)

Frequently the maps that a captain carried had been drawn especially for his particular voyage. John Dee is thought to have designed the map that Humphrey Gilbert sent to Queen Elizabeth along with his *Discourse of a Discoverie for a new Passage to Cataia* and his request for letters patent for northwest exploration. It bears Gilbert's arms and motto (*Quid Non*) and is labeled "A General Map, made onelye for the Particular Declaration of this Discourse."

In addition to his maps, every pilot guarded a collection of what in northern Europe were called rutters (from the French word for route) and in southern Europe, portulans. These rutters or portulans contained directions for getting from one place to another. They also indicated depths of high water during a new or full moon at various headlands, channels, and ports as well as soundings at principal havens. On capturing a ship, a captain hastened to confiscate such documents; even though he might himself have made the voyages they described, they might reveal some bit of information unknown to him, and confiscation would, in any case, deprive an enemy of their use. Nuño da Silva, a Portuguese pilot whom Drake kept prisoner in 1578, wrote of Drake, "the first thing he did when he had captured a vessel was to seize the charts, astrolabes and mariner's compasses which he broke and cast into the sea."

Many chart rooms contained not only terrestrial charts (charts of the earth) but also celestial charts (charts of the heavens), by which pilots related their course to the annual procession of sun and stars. The best instrument makers had begun to offer terrestrial and celestial globes in pairs. The celestial charts marked the equinoctial (the heavenly equator) midway between the two celestial poles, across which the sun's path (the ecliptic) moves during the spring and fall equinoxes. They showed such constellations as Ursa Major, the Great Bear (popularly called the Big Dipper in America, the Wain or the Plow in England), whose two front stars are known as the pointers because they point to the North Star; Ursa Minor, the Little Bear (or the Little Dipper), in whose bowl the two brightest stars are known as the Guardians of the Pole or the Guards of the North Star; and the twelve signs of the Zodiac, one for each month of the year, located in a belt 6 degrees wide on each side of the equinoctial and designated by the astronomers as "fixed stars." The heavenly charts likewise supplied information on what were termed the "wandering stars"—the sun and

"Prognostications" were frequently issued along with navigator's tables. A detail from the title page of *A Prognostication Everlastinge . . .* (1576) by Leonard and his son Thomas Digges relates signs of the zodiac to parts of the human body. By permission of the Folger Shakespeare Library.

moon and the five visible planets, Mercury, Venus, Mars, Jupiter, and Saturn. As with the terrestrial charts, truly accurate use of the celestial charts was impossible without refinements not available at the time of the Roanoke voyages. Nevertheless, the charts were of great aid to mariners, both in guiding their ships and in keeping track of time.

Once a course was charted, the immemorial aid in following it was the compass. Sir Humphrey Gilbert took twenty such instruments with him on his voyage—a testament to the importance of the device. A compass (sometimes a pair of them) was kept in front of the helmsman in a brass or wooden box placed on a shelved cupboard first called the bittacle and later the binnacle. A mark—the lubber's line—on the rim of the compass indicated the fore-and-aft axis of the ship. To compensate for the ship's motion and keep the instrument level, the compass was usually placed on gimbals. Lodestones to activate compass needles were frequently enclosed in brass mountings with a ring by which a stone could be attached to a chain for safekeeping. Alongside the compass, the helmsman had a half-hour glass by which he kept the ship's time, turning the glass and striking the ship's bell at each half-hour. The ringing of the bell regulated the changing of the watch.

For the short trips of the European coastal trade, "compass cards," with lines drawn from one port to the other, ensured that the captain who held to the line would arrive at his destination. But on transatlantic voyages, use of the compass required corrections because a compass needle points to the magnetic pole rather than true north and does not do even that consistently. (On his first voyage, Columbus made special note of shifts.) Compasses showing deviations from true north were developed subsequently.

Even the best of captains could lose his bearings. William Bourne, warning against errors that the variation of a compass might cause, cites what happened to Drake when, following his 1585-1586 raids in the West Indies, he

put to sea for Virginia, for the reliefe of our Contreymen that were there in great danger and distresse: Hauing continued at the Sea sixteene dayes tossed with variable windes, they came at last within sight of land: but by no means could they discerne, or giue any probable ghesse what lande it should be.

Drake had in his company a man who, though then in disgrace with his commander, was a skilled navigator. Calling him into conference, Sir Francis indicated a willingness to forget the offense in return for nautical advice:

at length he vndertaketh to doe his best. And hauing made his obseruations according unto Arte, he pronounced in laughing and disdainefull maner (because his aduise was not taken in the setting of their course) that looke what land they had bin at sixteene days before, the very same precisely was the land that now they were at againe. VVhich assertion of his being reiected, as a thing impossible, by all those of skill in the company, and especially by Sir Francis himselfe not without reprochfull wordes; he still preseuered therein, and assured them, that vpon his life they should find it so; like as in the ende they did.

A pilot's best means of determining his latitude by observing the declination of the sun was by use of a cross-staff, a device that had been brought from the

Continent by Dr. Dee. By measuring the angle between the horizon and the sun's height at noon, he could calculate his distance north of the equator. The difficulty of getting an accurate reading from the deck of a small, pitching vessel was, however, considerable.

An alternative to the cross-staff for measuring the sun's elevation was the sea astrolabe, the simplified form of a much more elaborate scientific instrument that had been adapted to navigational use at Lisbon in the fifteenth century by the Nuremberg savant Martin Behaim. The nocturnal, less frequently carried than the astrolabe, was a similar instrument used to navigate by the stars.

The nautical mileage covered each day was an essential part of a ship's record. But the method used to estimate the distance a ship traveled was a rudimentary procedure. A log attached to a line was thrown overboard at the ship's bow, and a half-hour glass turned as the log hit the water. The glass measured the time until the ship's stern passed the log. Given the known length of the ship and the time it required to sail that distance on the current wind, a rough figure of the ship's speed could be calculated. A traverse board beside the helmsman permitted him to peg the number of hours the ship traveled on each wind that occurred during a twenty-four-hour period. From these data an estimate of each day's run was compiled.

On approach to a port or an unknown shore, a captain used a lead and line to take soundings. Each time the line was drawn up, a sailor counted the knots that were tied in the line at one-fathom intervals and called out the depth. He also looked at the tallow on the sinker at the line's end for a sample of the

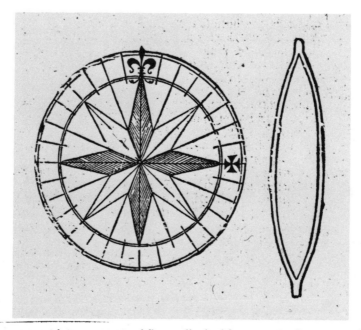

The compass, with its magnetized fly needle, had for centuries been a standard navigational instrument. From Eden, *Arte of Navigation*, edition of 1596, f. 61; by permission of the Folger Shakespeare Library.

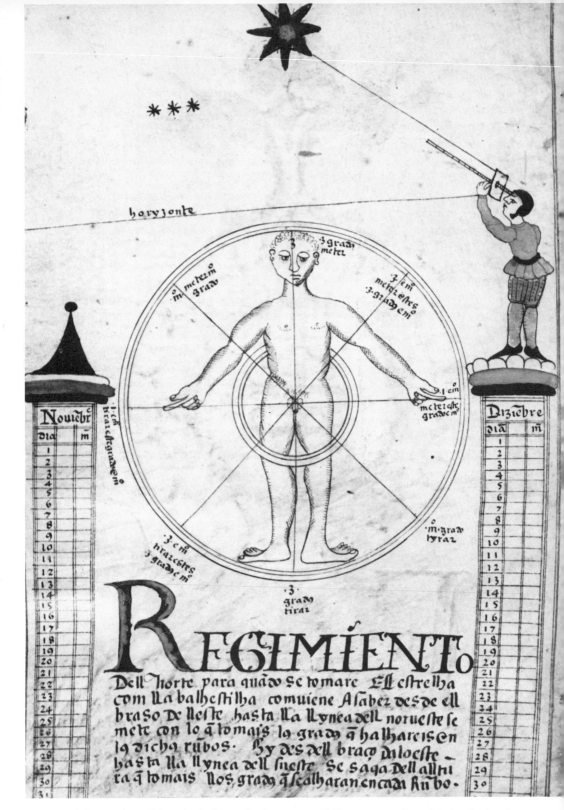

The cross-staff, by which the sun's elevation could be measured, enabled a ship's pilot to determine latitude. From Portulan Atlas No. 14, f. 15v; The Maritime Museum, London.

bottom—mud, sand, rock, coral—at the place where anchorage was anticipated.

As hostilities between Spain and England intensified, artists sketched profiles of likely landfalls in the West Indies to help intruding English captains avoid clashes with the Spanish. Using the sketches to identify islands from a distance by the shapes of hills or promontories, English captains had time to consider alternative landing sites in their inevitable search for water.

Even before writing his *Regiment for the Sea*, William Bourne published a series of almanacs containing data that mariners needed to interpret readings on some of their instruments. Included were tables of the sun's declination, information on positions of a few stars, and rules for use of the North Star. The almanacs had calendars showing phases of the moon to allow calculation of spring (high) tides and neap (low) tides. They also contained tide tables for ports of shallow draft where entry on high tide was a condition of safety. As seamen increased their understanding of mathematical tables, enlarged almanacs and "prognostications" became popular.

The prognostications featured in the titles of these publications titilated a public still credulous of the magical experiments of the scientists of the period; like all oracles, they were loosely enough phrased for many of them to be cited as prophetic after an event had occurred. Readers of the prognostications for 1585 contained in two popular publications, Thomas Porter's *An almanacke or prognostication for the years . . . M.D.LXXXV* or Evan Lloyd's *An almanacke and prognostication for this present yeare . . . 1585,* might claim in hindsight that they anticipated the outcome of Ralegh's first venture. Porter's almanac warned:

Item, yf any man hath many Iourneys to take by land or by water, let hym haue an eye rounde about hym, for Force is lykely to exceede in all places, and Violence already shaketh his head, and frowneth vpon Trauaylers: but warinesse and courage, are the best spelles agaynst such Sprites and Goblins.

Lloyd also cautioned: "Moreouer, discoueries this yeare attempted, are like to prove but badly: and the trauellers to sustaine great labour and trouble therein, and to returne with but small gaine or much losse."

In addition to skill in using the various navigational instruments, pilots needed the wisdom born of actual experience at sea to set a ship's course. This necessity accounted in large part for the condescension with which pilots of many past voyages viewed land-based compilers of cosine tables and devisers of celestial astrolabes.

After only a few decades of transatlantic trafficking, mariners had experienced and charted the prevailing winds and currents of the North and South Atlantic. These soon were consolidated into westbound and eastbound courses that almost all ships followed. The reduction of mileage offered by great circle sailing (following a course that takes advantage of the fact that the shortest distance between two points on the surface of a sphere is along the arc of a great circle) had been recognized in the first half of the sixteenth century by the cosmographer to the king of Portugal, but for sailing ships, the time a captain saved with a reliably good wind at his back could be more important than the distance he had to cover to take advantage of it.

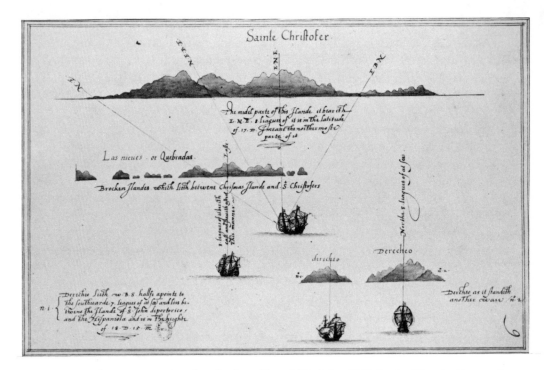

Sixteenth-century artists sketched profiles of likely landfalls in the West Indies, such as this one of the island of Saint Christopher, to help English sea captains avoid clashes with the Spanish. From Ch. de la Roncière (ed.), *Un Atlas Inconnu de la dernière Expédition de Drake* (Paris: Imprimerie Nationale, 1909), f. 9; Bibliothéque Nationale, Paris.

From England, the usual course to the mid-American coast was a long way round. In order to reach the swift and steady trade winds, blowing up and across the Atlantic from Africa, English ships sailed south from their home ports at least as far as the Canaries, and often to the Cape Verde Islands. Turning west there after refilling their water casks, they were assured of a reasonably constant wind that (with the prevailing current) would speed them across the Atlantic to the West Indies.

The West Indies were Spanish territory. But because no ship could go farther without revictualing, rewatering, and usually repairing, and because Spain could only sporadically police so vast an area, English captains usually made several stops in the Indies, sometimes of considerable length. Illegal traders of assorted nationalities had hideouts in the islands and carried on profitable exchange. Once a fleet was refreshed, it turned northwest to take advantage of the Bahama current and the Florida current, which became the Gulf Stream, flowing along the American coast as far north as Cape Hatteras.

On the return voyage, the ships took an entirely different, much more northerly route, avoiding the thick and clinging yellow weed of the Sargasso Sea

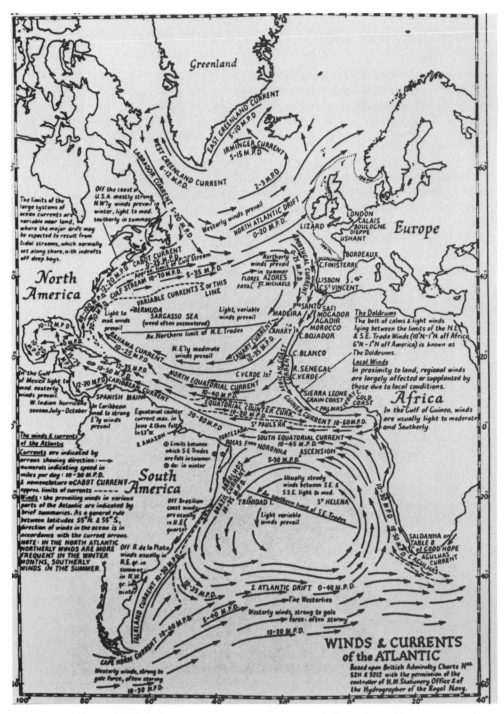

Elizabethan mariners soon became familiar with the winds and currents of the Atlantic and set their courses accordingly. From David W. Waters, *The Art of Navigation in Elizabethan and Early Stuart Times* (London: Trustees of The National Maritime Museum, 1958), facing p. 265; by kind permission of Lt. Commander David W. Waters, Royal Navy.

and the frequent calms there. Swinging across the North Atlantic with the Gulf Stream, they watered and revictualed in the harbors of the Azores before departing for their home ports. Richard Hakluyt's written descriptions of "Markes" helped either outbound or homebound ships to identify major islands, supplementing the profile sketches also carried on board. Because the islands of Fayal and Flores in the Azores were where many ships watered—and where English privateers often laid in wait for Spanish treasure fleets and Portuguese East India cargoes—Hakluyt's descriptions of them were particularly useful. Over these routes, outbound and homebound, a growing number of English began to practice an increasing mastery of the sea. A western passage that at its end would touch the desired land was not yet a reliable certainty. But it was no longer a bare hypothesis.

IV. The Ship's Company

When prospective planters came aboard an English ship, they entered a new community. Those whose families were seafarers took the social structure of a ship for granted; to others, the organization of the vessel as a complete society in miniature could well have come as a surprise. A chain of command, forged by English law and the custom of the sea, encircled the ship and bound it together, from the humblest grommet (apprentice) to the captain-general. In such a company the colonists were but passive participants, spectators of those who kept the ship on its course; but in that capacity they had ample opportunity to observe both the duties and the personalities of the men who operated the vessel.

The captain-general of a fleet was not only the leader of the expedition but also the representative of his sovereign and the governor responsible for law and order. He was more often than not a man of military rather than navigational experience, though most of the ranking captains were seafarers as well as veterans of campaigns with the queen's armies in Ireland and on the Continent and many were experienced in sea battles as well as engagements on land. Sir Richard Grenville, leader of Ralegh's first colony, was among those doubly qualified.

The captain-general's judicial authority prevailed over all on board and covered the entire range of offenses. Sentences were harsh. The punishment for capital crimes such as treason or mutiny—crimes that occurred all too frequently during early and unfamiliar voyages—could be execution or abandonment on an alien shore. When rounding Cape Horn, Sir Francis Drake executed Thomas Doughty, private secretary to the queen's vice-chamberlain, on a charge of conspiracy. Then, in an exceptional assumption of the queen's authority as head of the church, Drake temporarily excommunicated the fleet's chaplain and artist, Francis Fletcher, for attributing a difficult situation in which the expedition shortly found itself to the Creator's disapproval of Doughty's sentence.

In the eyes of the captain-general, a crew could be as intractible as Sir Richard Hawkins found his to be when he noted: "Mariners are like to a stiff-necked horse, which taking a bridle betwixt his teeth, forced his rider to what his list, mauger his will." Sebastian Cabot's specifications for behavior of crew members, set forth at the beginning of England's entry into transoceanic navigation and repeated in various forms thereafter, support a similar estimate, warning that there must be no blaspheming of God, or detestable swearing to be used in any ship, nor communication of ribaldrie, filthy tales, or ungodly talke to be suffred in the company of any ship, neither dicing, carding, tabling, nor other divelish games to be frequented, whereby ensueth not onely povertie to the players, but also strife, variance, brauling, fighting, and oftentimes murther to the utter destruction of the parties. . . .

The Elizabethan seaman's dress included a warm hat to protect against loss of body heat when a sailor worked aloft in rain and cold weather. From Cesare Vecelli, *Habiti Antichi e Moderni* (1600), f. 285v; by permission of the Folger Shakespeare Library.

In the case of murder of one crew member by another, the guilty sailor was tied, alive, to the corpse of the man he had killed and both were thrown overboard. Sentences for lesser crimes included keelhauling, with the condemned man thrown overboard at the ship's bow and drawn the length of the ship by two crew members with a rope attached to him on either side. He was rarely alive when pulled up at the stern. Another punishment was flogging at the mast, with the boatswain seeing to it that the number of stripes the sentence required to be laid on a seaman's bare back were heartily delivered. Tongue scraping was imposed if the charge was blasphemy.

The captain-general was also the commander of the soldiers and gunners carried by most ships in anticipation of sea fights and privateering captures. Rules of conduct proposed for such members of Sir Walter Ralegh's 1585 expedition were comparably strict, including regulations to govern their conduct toward Indians:

First that no Souldier do violat any woman, 2 That no Souldier do take any mans goodes forcibly from hym. 3 That no Indian be forced to labor unwillyngly. 4 That no Souldier shall defraud her Maieste of her fyfte. [In the case of privateering spoils, the queen expected and usually obtained a fifth of all gold, silver, and jewels taken on the voyage, together with a 5 percent duty on all commodities.] 5 That no Souldier abbandon his ensegne without leave, of his Capten, 6 That non shall stryke or misuse any Indian. 7 That non shall Enter any Indian's howse without his leave, 8 That non shall stryke within the forte nor fytt within a myll of It. 9 That non offer to draw any weapon uppon any Conselor or his Captain, 10 That no Souldier sleep in sentenell or abbandon his sentenell or garde.

For the breach of these rules, the punishments suggested were:

To the fyrst deathe, To the second a dubbell restutution, if the souldier be not abell, to have a years Imprisonment the whype and bannishement or condemd to the gallys for vij years. and the party to have his restutition of the. Prince. To the, 3. iij monthes Imprisonment, to the. 4. deathe or a perpetuall Condemnation to the gallys or myns, to the 5 deathe or vij yeres Slavery to the 6, to have xx blows with a cuggell In the presentz of the Indian strucken. To the .7. vj monthes imprisonment or slavery To the .8. lose of hand. To the .9. & 10th present deathe without remission.

The captain-general's civil and military authority was paralleled by the authority of his second-in-command, the admiral, and by the navigational authority of the chief pilot of the fleet, the latter chosen for his experience acquired during previous voyages and his skill in the use of navigational instruments. The chief pilot was the officer responsible for the movement of the ships until all aboard were safely berthed at their destination. Masters in charge of individual vessels gave instructions to their helmsmen in respect to the course and to their boatswains on making and furling sail and day-to-day operation. The boatswains, usually men of awesome physique and penetrating voice, ruled the mariners. The shrill sound of the whistle, which was the boatswain's badge of office, brought crew members to their designated stations on the double.

During the years when the English were catching up with the Spanish and Portuguese in exploring the Atlantic Ocean, chief pilots of English ships were frequently nationals of Spain and Portugal. Even later, when English captains captured Spanish or Portuguese prizes, they usually kept the pilots as prisoners in order to take advantage of their familiarity with West Indian and other harbors.

Simon Fernandes or Ferdinando, a Portuguese born on the Azores island of Terceira and trained first in Portugal and then at the Spanish Casa de Contratación in Seville, spent a good part of his life in the English service. He came with wide experience gained during voyages to the Orient, to South America, and on Spanish expeditions up the North American coast. He entered English records as a successful pirate in the waters between the English Channel and the Azores and brought his captured goods to the English West Country for disposal. Arrested at Cardiff, he was dismissed on a reduced charge of "suspicion of piracy" at the initiative of Francis Walsingham, the queen's principal secretary and head of her secret service, in whose employ he remained thereafter. Settling and marrying in London and joining the Church of England, Fernandes eventually ranked as a merchant and a gentleman. The Spanish high admiral, the duke of Medina Sidonia, declared him to be one of the best pilots in England. Spain's resident ambassador there denounced him as a "thorough-going scoundrel."

In the 1570s Fernandes began a long association with Sir Humphrey Gilbert and Walter Ralegh. He was chief pilot on Gilbert's expedition of 1578, sailing on the ship commanded by Ralegh, and was leader of the 1580 reconnaissance for Gilbert's 1583 venture. (He missed the 1583 voyage because he was engaged in piloting a fruitless excursion begun by Edward Fenton in 1582.) He was chief pilot for all the Ralegh voyages, from Amadas and Barlowe's exploratory trip in 1584 to the planting of the second colony in 1587.

Partly for their own comfort and partly to impress any Spanish, Portuguese, or native dignitaries whom they might entertain en route, the captain-general and admiral of a fleet were well quartered. Frequently, though not always, they sailed on different ships. Their cabins in the sterncastle were equipped with fine furniture—beds, sideboards, tables, and chairs. The captain-general was responsible for the supply of his own table; his meals were elegantly served, often on silver plate.

Almost as well accommodated as the leaders, sharing their social status, and bringing page boys along to attend them were the passengers designated as "Gentlemen." Sometimes they were backers of the voyage, sometimes aristocratic younger sons desirous of learning the ways of the sea. As part of the Roanoke voyage of 1585, the future circumnavigator Thomas Cavendish came in command of his own ship, the *Elizabeth*. Aboard Spanish vessels, these grandees were merely passengers who took no part in the ship's functioning; but Drake held that in times of crisis it was up to such passengers to lend a hand: "I must have the gentleman to draw with the mariner . . . and the mariner with the gentleman."

A Spanish impression of the manner in which some English captains-general traveled has come down from Don Francisco de Zarate, a cousin of the duke of Medina Sidonia. He was captured by Drake during his circumnavigation and lodged aboard the *Golden Hind*:

His [Drake's] vessel is . . . a perfect sailer. She is manned with a hundred men all of service and of an age for warfare, and all are as practised therein as old soldiers could be. Each one takes particular pains to keep his arquebus clean. He treats them with affection and they treat him with respect. He carries with him nine or ten cavaliers, cadets of English noblemen. . . .

He is served on silver dishes with gold borders and gilded garlands, in which are his arms. He carries all possible dainties and perfumed waters. He said that many of these had been given him by the Queen. . . .

He dines and sups to the music of viols. . . . I understood that all the men he carries with him receive wages, because when our ship was sacked, no man dared take anything without his orders. He shows them great favour, but punishes the least fault. He also carries painters who paint for him pictures of the coast in its exact colours. This I was most grieved to see, for each thing is so naturally depicted that no one who guides himself according to these paintings can possibly go astray.

Expeditions commanded by their elders also gave younger relatives opportunities to gain experience: Thomas, youngest of the twelve Drake boys, of whom Francis was the eldest, sailed on most of Francis's voyages. Francis Drake himself had made his first transatlantic voyage on an expedition with his Hawkins relatives. In turn, two of Drake's younger relatives, John and Richard Hawkins, acquired seafaring experience by accompanying him on various voyages. John sailed around the world, and Richard commanded the galliot *Duck* on Drake's 1585-1586 expedition to the West Indies. On each of Sir Humphrey Gilbert's colonizing expeditions, his younger half brother, Walter Ralegh, received a command, though in the end Ralegh did not make the second journey.

On voyages of exploration and attempts at settlement, the flagship's sterncastle housed scientists like Thomas Harriot who were charged with bringing back detailed accounts of the physical characteristics and flora and fauna of the places visited, describing new peoples, and preparing maps. Jacques le Moyne de Morgues's watercolors of the Huguenot expedition to Florida under Captain René Goulaine de Laudonnière in 1564, together with John White's paintings at Roanoke, are the earliest foreign portrayals of native American life. Nuño da Silva reported that Drake "carries a book in which he writes his log and paints birds, trees, and animals. He is diligent in painting and carries along a boy [Drake's nephew John] . . . who is a great painter; shut up in his cabin they were always painting." Similarly, Thomas Cavendish, when he went round the world, took with him Harriot's mathematical friend Robert Hues, who dedicated his *Tractatus de Globus et eorum Usu* to Ralegh. Other members of a ship's company who usually lodged in the sterncastle were the chaplain, the surgeon, and the apothecary.

Divine services were a regular part of a ship's routine, with a sermon for all hands on Sunday and morning and evening prayers several times a week. Chaplains had no hesitation in offering moral guidance to commanders as well as seamen. During Captain Edward Fenton's voyage of 1582-1583 that set out for China but went no farther than the South American coast, Simon Fernandes's improper language troubled John Walker, one of the chaplains, sufficiently for him to take up with Fenton the need to get the man to watch his tongue.

Richard Madox, Fenton's other chaplain, kept, partly in private cipher, a very frank diary in which the identities of his shipmates were disguised by classical names. His bombastic entries corroborate Walker's views of Fernandes:

So much does the expert pronounce about these matters . . . and wish to die by hanging and to be thrust with the lowest shades of the departed if those thousand discoveries are not equally reliable and certain as the oracle of Apollo or the gospels themselves. And so our own Fernando is wont to do: . . . they come out disguised in a swill of many languages and everywhere abound in barbarisms, solecisms and hyperbatons; these he sells as his own and boasts of himself as a notable author and inventor when rather he should be called a perverter of books, an extorter of readers, and a tormentor of writers. In these books nothing else is contained but trivialities and vulgarities and what the wit of a sailor would know, dull, obtuse and, what is worse and almost common to all of his class, rash and stubborn and intolerant of all instruction and learning.

The surgeon and the apothecary might sleep in the sterncastle, but successive emergencies claimed most of their time in the stifling little operating room at the bottom of the hold. There, following external injuries to sailors and soldiers during sea battles, shore landings, or skirmishes with hostile natives, the surgeon sawed mangled limbs into usable stumps, sewed up lacerations, extracted splinters, cut out arrow tips. Since antiseptics were unknown, all operations were high risks. Available anesthesia was confined to the "soporific sponge" given to a patient to inhale; its contents included opium, hycocyamus, hemlock, mandragora, and lettuce, mulberry, and ivy juice. Knowledge was being imported from the Continent, and instrument makers sold surgeon's kits. Mostly, however, surgeons worked by rule of thumb: instruction in anatomy and pathology, such as that given by John Banester at London's Barber-Surgeon's Hall, was a pioneering novelty.

Because of the rivalry between the Royal College of Physicians and the Barber-Surgeons Company, on whose members the college looked down, surgeons were not authorized to practice internal medicine. Banester's permission to do so came only through the direct intervention of the queen. Yet internal ailments, such as the bloody flux, brought aboard at the start of a voyage or acquired from lack of sanitation later, often reached epidemic proportions. Tropical diseases unfamiliar in Britain, such as malaria, were picked up at stops en route. On long voyages, scurvy debilitated and decimated crews whose diet, month after month, was limited to sea rations. There were frequent instances when disease rendered a ship unmanageable or forced its return to port.

Few physicians ever went to sea; nor did they follow up the observant suggestions of experienced mariners. As early as 1572 a captain noticed that mosquito bites and malaria apparently were related, but the causal relationship was not scientifically confirmed for over 350 years. Quinine did not become a remedy until the eighteenth century. Writing after he had visited the Pacific in 1593, Sir Richard Hawkins set down a detailed description of the grim course of scurvy and estimated that 10,000 seamen died of it in Elizabeth's time. Venturing the view that prevention was to be found in citrus fruit, he wrote: "This is a wonderful secret of the power and wisdom of God, that hath hidden so great and unknown a virtue in this fruit, to be a certain remedy for this infirmity." A decade later, Sir James Lancaster, on a voyage to India, kept his flagship free from the disease by administering a spoonful of lemon juice to crew members each morning. (But the cause of scurvy as a deficiency of Vitamin C was not verified by experimental medicine until 1932.)

The forecastle was the boatswain's territory. Loading and unloading, lowering and raising anchors, setting and reefing sails, manning longboats, preparing the ship's mess, filling water casks, repairing hull and canvas after storms or enemy action were among the tasks performed under his immediate supervision; and most boatswains were attentive taskmasters.

As to quarters, while top specialists in the crew might bunk in the forecastle with the boatswain, the ordinary seamen, the grommets, and the boys slept where they could, in the hold or on the open deck. With the day divided into 5 watches of 4 hours and 2 watches of 2 hours, sleep was in any case sporadic.

Lists of the period show the number of specialists, from carpenter to cook, with their mates and apprentices, and the various grades of seamen who served on the average ship. When Richard Chancellor sailed aboard the *Edward Bonaventura*, a vessel of 160 tons, there were, besides himself as captain-general and chief pilot of the expedition and Stephen Borough, master, a master's mate, a minister, a master gunner, a gunner's mate, two gunners, a surgeon, a boatswain, a boatswain's mate, four quartermasters, a steward, a steward's mate, a cook, a cooper, a carpenter, and 21 sailors, including grommets. These men were the bone and sinew of the fleet. A normal ratio of crew to tonnage was in the range of one crewman per four to five tons; for tropical voyages with a high death rate, one per two tons.

The key to a successful transoceanic voyage was the number of seasoned mariners aboard. As was the case with their commanders, the ships' crews came largely from the counties of Britain's southwest peninsula. A 1582 muster roll of seamen put Devon and Cornwall's combined total enumeration at 5,009. A 1583 census of the maritime population of England, excluding Wales, showed 1,484 masters, 11,515 mariners, 2,299 fishermen (normally exempt from other sea services), and 959 Thames wherrymen.

But not all who sailed on the long voyages did so willingly. Throughout the Elizabethan period, crews were partially composed of men swept on board by press gangs. For certain voyages, justices of the peace under royal authorization issued orders for the impressment of the numbers required. More often than not, the bodies provided included the weak and the sick and those who, according to their more able companions, "didn't know a rope." Sir Richard Hawkins described the process of impressment for one of his voyages:

And so I began to gather my company on board, which occupied my good friends and the Justices of the town two days, and forced us to search all lodgings, taverns and alehouses. For some would ever be taking their leave and never depart; some drink themselves so drunk that except they were carried aboard, they of themselves would not be able to go one step; others knowing the necessity of the time, feigned themselves sick; others to be indebted to their hosts, and forced me to ransom them.

Whatever service impressed seamen rendered usually masked a preoccupation with escape at the first opportunity.

John Banester's lectures on anatomy at the London hall of the Barber-Surgeons Company improved the knowledge and skill of the members who shipped for sea duty. From MS Hunter 364; courtesy of the Librarian, Glasgow University Library.

The unpopularity of sea service had many grounds. While pay scales were roughly comparable to those for work on land, payment to returning crews was often tardy. Conditions of work, especially because of the quality of the food or the insufficiency of it, were frequently bad enough to cause mutinies. The victualing of ships was subject to much sharp practice. Seamen messed in groups of four; each sailor was entitled to a daily ration of a pound of biscuit, a gallon of beer (issued a quart at a time, four times a day), a pound of salt meat on four days of each week, and dried fish and cheese on the other three. But deliveries were often short and casks leaky. When delivered, the biscuit was often moldy, meat maggoty, beer watery, and water, especially when it grew scarce, alive with wigglers.

In *A generall rehearsall of warres, wherein is five hundred severall services of land and sea,* Thomas Churchyard's description of a "gentleman of a verre good house" who had turned pirate, suggests how most seamen looked:

With horie beard and scorched face
With poudred hedde, and heare unshorn;
With hackes and hewes, in every place,
He seemed like, a man forlorne.

His lippes and cheeks, were pale and thinne,
His hollowed eyes, were sonke in hedde;
His fleshe was frette, nought left but skinne,
His marrowe dried, that youth had bredde.

His teeth and gummes, like harowes stood,
His furrowed face, like ploughed land;
His vaines did want, their wonted bloode,
His sinewes shronke, like knottes did stande.

A Sea mans cappe, on hedde he ware,
A slidying sloppe of Friers graie;
A checker Kaep, both thinne and bare,
To furnish up, his quaint araie.

A gables end, his girdle made,
His shurt besmerde, with Pitche and Tarre,
Close by his side, a rustie blade,
This carle in youth, a man of warre.

A Pilotes compasse, he did holde,
To showe what science he profest.
The skill whereof, had made hym bolde,
To saile the seas, both East and West.

If mariners' tavern tales of sea hazards that they had survived were often exaggerated, the grimness of the actual events of John White's return from Roanoke Island in 1587 was real enough. At departure time on August 28, twelve of his crew stepped to the capstan to wind up the pinnace's 750-pound anchor, but the anchor's flukes had snagged. As they pushed, one of the three spokes on the capstan snapped; the other two slammed backward across the chests of the mariners, mortally maiming a number of them. Though this anchor was his last—he had previously lost his others in the Caribbean—the master had to order the hawser cut when the strength of the men remaining uninjured proved incapable of freeing the anchor.

White reached the Azores with only five men fit for work; he picked up additional crew there, but the next twenty days saw small progress in light winds. Supplies, especially of water, dwindled to the danger point; crewmen sickened and two died. Then suddenly, out of the northeast, roared so violent a gale that for six days they could only flee before it. The lost distance took thirteen days to recover.

On October 16 White and his crew sighted unfamiliar land; it turned out to be Ireland's Dingle peninsula. They had lost their longboat, so they could not row into harbor. Until help came, the anchorless ship wallowed. Three sick sailors were taken ashore, and the boatswain, his mate, and a steward died on board. It was November 8, seventy-two days after sailing, before they reached an English port.

The future awaiting the cripples in White's crew is vividly shown by two wooden statues in the Great Hall of St. Bartholomew's Hospital in London. Seriously injured seamen had little choice, once ashore, but to join the "divers dissolute and idle persons, Rogues, Vagabonds and Sturdy Beggars . . . [who] do continue to wander up and down, pilfering and begging through all Parts of the Kingdom"; against such persons the Elizabethan Poor Law was enacted in 1601. With the closing of monasteries following Henry VIII's break with Rome, the hospices in which nuns and friars cared for sick and indigent persons disappeared. A measure of relief was offered by the Trinity Houses founded by the same king, and by charitable chests set up by various private citizens. In 1590 Drake, Hawkins, and others established the Chatham Chest, whose strongbox can be seen today in the Queen's House at Greenwich. But despite these efforts, far less relief was available than was needed.

Grisly tales of seamen's sufferings as captives were no less real than those of losing encounters with the anger of the sea. John Hortop, powder maker, was impressed as a gunner for the *Jesus of Lubeck* in John Hawkins's ill-fated expedition to the Gulf of Mexico. He sailed in October, 1567, and was not seen again in England until he returned to his home in Redriffe near London on Christmas eve, 1590. His deposition on his twenty-three years of absence lists most of the misfortunes and calamities that could happen to a sailor in the hands of the Spanish enemy.

Hortop's sufferings began when Hawkins, sailing away in his *Minion* from his defeat at San Juan de Ullua, picked up Hortop along with other survivors of the abandoned *Jesus of Lubeck*. Aboard the *Minion* the overcrowded men "were driven to eate hides, cats, rats, parrats, munkies and doggies." When Hortop and ninety-six others said that they had rather be on shore to shift for themselves amid the enemy, Hawkins landed them. They wandered for a week, alternately meeting friendly and hostile Indians and losing men. Robbed of their clothing, Hortop recalled, "we made wreaths of greene grasse, which we wound about our bodies, to keepe us from the Sunne, and gnats of that Countrey." Captured by Spanish horsemen, they were taken to Mexico to appear before the viceroy; there, escaping a threatened hanging by asserting that they were Catholics, they were assigned to card wool among Indian slaves.

Two years later, while dispatched for Spain in a fleet that joined the treasure flota, two of them gained momentary Spanish gratitude by saving the entire expedition. Rounding Florida, the Spanish pilot "had like to have cast away the fleet upon the Cape called Cannaveral, which was prevented by me John Hortop, & our master Robert Barrett; for I being in the second watch escried land, and called to Robert Barrett, bidding him looke over board, for I saw land under the lee-bow of the ship: he called to the boatswaine, & bid him let flie the fore saile sheat, and lay the helm upon the lee, and cast the ship about. . . . For

Sir John Hawkins, of the Plymouth family of merchants and sea captains, greatly influenced the design of English ships after he became Elizabeth's navy treasurer in 1578. From Henry Holland, *Herwologia Anglica* (1620), facing p. 100; by permission of the Folger Shakespeare Library.

this we were beloved of the Generall, and all the fleet."

But at Fayal in the Azores, when Hortop and his fellow crewmen were discovered planning to escape by stealing a pinnace, they were ordered to be collectively hanged from the yardarms. In a last-minute reprieve, the fleet's admiral, Diego Flores de Valdes, countermanded the execution and ordered the prisoners brought to Seville.

Imprisoned there for a year, seven of them, including Hortop, escaped. After being recaptured, they underwent an additional year of imprisonment before being led to a scaffold in the town square. There Robert Barrett and one other were burned alive. Hortop and the rest were sentenced to row in the galleys of Spain's Mediterranean trade.

He survived twelve years at the oars. "We were chained," he testified, "foure and foure together: every mans daily allowance was 26. ounces of course blacke bisket and water ... our lodging was on the bare boords, and banks of the Gallies, our heads and beards were shaven every month, hunger, thirst, cold and stripes we lacked none." Then, returned to Seville, he "was sent to the everlasting prison remedilesse." Four years later, after a promise to serve for seven years as a slave, Hortop bribed his way into the household of the treasurer of the king's mint. In October, 1590, he managed to slip away from the nearby port of San Lucár in a Flemish boat. Off Cape Finesterre, the English galleon *Dudley* captured the vessel. And so Hortop came home.

Many who sailed did not come home at all. When Drake brought the *Golden Hind* into the River Thames to receive his knighthood in Queen Elizabeth's presence after circumnavigating the world, only fifteen of his original crew were present as survivors of the voyage. Yet, in the English towns and counties where the plague had inured inhabitants to the passage of corpse-collecting wagons, the mortality rate at sea probably seemed unsurprising. Certainly, some of the popular songs like the merry ditty *Britons, strike home* took it for granted.

> Our ship carried over nine hundred men,
> And out of nine hundred, five hundred were slain;
> for we range the wild seas
> Where the wind blows so strong,
> While our rakish young heroes cry,
> "Britons, strike home, my boys,"
> Cry, "Britons, strike home."

Though for the most part they lived longer than their crews, mortality struck the great captains with equal force. Sir Humphrey Gilbert disappeared with his little *Squirrel* in a violent North Atlantic storm in 1583. Sir Richard Grenville went down with the *Revenge* while attempting to sail her through the middle of a Spanish fleet in 1591. Sir Martin Frobisher, wounded and attended by an unskillful surgeon when landing troops on the Continent in 1594, faltered back to Plymouth to die, his entrails buried there in St. Andrew's, his other remains in London's St. Giles Cripplegate. During their Caribbean expedition of 1595, both Sir John Hawkins and Sir Francis Drake were buried at sea when they perished from tropical disease. In 1618, by order of King James I, Sir Walter Ralegh was executed in London's Old Palace Yard. His head, in a leather bag, was handed to his widow and the rest of his body laid in the chancel of St. Margaret's, Westminster.

Yet, a core element of the crews that sailed during the last quarter of the sixteenth century went to sea with a zest that differed little from that of their commanders and was often induced by admiration for them. Able and ambitious youths who shipped before the mast during earlier voyages occasionally became captains in their own right. Peter Pett of Essex, who was

Sir Martin Frobisher, English navigator, explorer, and commander of the *Triumph* against the Spanish Armada in 1588, served as vice admiral of Sir Francis Drake's fleet that stopped at Roanoke Island in 1586. From Holland, *Herwologia Anglica* (1620), plate 96; by permission of the Folger Shakespeare Library.

forced into his first experience at sea by a press gang, returned to found the Deptford dynasty of the Pett family, England's ranking firm of shipbuilders for a century to come. William Borough of Appledore and Bideford, who learned ocean navigation as a common seaman under his brother Stephen, master of Richard Chancellor's *Edward Bonaventura*, rose to be chief pilot of the Muscovy Company and later joined with Sir John Hawkins to improve ship design and naval administration in the queen's service. Christopher Newport, of Limehouse on the River Thames, went to sea as a common mariner in 1581. In 1592 he was entrusted to bring into Dartmouth harbor the greatest prize the English ever captured, the 1,600-ton Portuguese *Madre de Diós*, taken on her way home from the Far East. In 1607, Newport captained the fleet that founded

Jamestown. Thus for some—even for a number of those who had been impressed—the sea became a way of life that united a considerable part of the ship's company by bonds other than the law-and-force of the rule book. Such bonds had several strands. There was the physical excitement of sailing into the unknown, contending with an element that all too often, they knew, would prove stronger than they. As nationalism replaced feudalism, the old tie between lord and vassal enlarged into an island-wide relationship between sovereign and subject. The claiming of new discoveries in the name of the queen and the spread of the English empire became a common cause.

At the same time, English mariners realized that service to that cause offered possibilities of personal as well as public profit; moments of triumph brought pecuniary rewards to participating crews as well as to queen and country. The financial ratios were well understood. First, 5 percent of the profits of a voyage (apart from 20 percent of the bullion and jewels) accrued to Elizabeth, and one tenth of 5 percent to her lord high admiral. Then came a division of the remainder into thirds—one for the expedition's organizer and backers, one for the victuallers who supplied it, and one for the ship's company. That final third was then divided into parts, with the number of parts payable to each of those on board specified in advance according to rank. The captain received nine parts, the master seven parts, and so on down to the ship's boys, who received one part each.

If the captured ships contained only humdrum loads of such merchandise as hides or sugar, the crew's share would not make its men rich. But when Drake returned to England after rounding the world, his renaming of his ship from *Pelican* to *Golden Hind* seemed symbolic, and thereafter the goddess of chance beckoned with a metallic glitter. Among common seamen, the glitter spread when Drake's nephew John received from his uncle a heavy gold chain for sighting the spice-laden Portuguese *Cacafuego*. The cargo of this imposing freighter was valued at £100,000. Overall, those who had contributed to that voyage—the queen and her courtiers Leicester, Hatton, and Walsingham, among others—profited at a rate of £47 received for each £1 advanced. With £3,400 of his royal award Drake completed his purchase of Grenville's country seat at Buckland Abbey. The crew members, dividing £8,000 while clamoring for more, each received sums that compared with a year's pay.

The prize of the century, the *Madre de Diós*, taken by the English off the Azores, was initially engaged by Sir John Burgh's *Foresight* and Ralegh's *Roebuck*, then assisted by ships of the earl of Cumberland. Seven decks deep, the captured ship was the victim of looting even before she was brought into port at Dartmouth.

While customs officials galloped down from Exeter, the spreading news brought some 2,000 lustful buyers swarming into Dartmouth. Learning that pearls and precious stones could be had by the handful, London jewelers lathered their horses. Professional pirates had no need to go to sea. Sailors in local alehouses were happy to exchange a finely carved piece of amber for a tankard. One naval officer admitted getting 1,800 diamonds and 300 rubies for

Caca Fogo.   Caca Plata.

Sir Francis Drake's capture of the Portuguese *Cacafuego*. (Coping with three languages, the German engraver Levinus Hulsius of Nuremberg confused his metals: he labeled the *Cacafuego* [the *Spitfire*] correctly but put *La Plata* [the *Silver*] under the *Golden Hind*.) Rare Books and Manuscripts Division, New York Public Library, Astor, Lenox, and Tilden Foundations.

£130. As the looting got further and further out of hand, Sir John Hawkins importuned the Privy Council, which already had sent the diminutive Robert Cecil, son of the queen's high treasurer, to restore order and protect the queen's share, to dispatch to Dartmouth the only man who could force the looters to cease and desist—Walter Ralegh.

Dartmouth Harbor, when the captured Portuguese *Madre de Dios* was brought there loaded with Oriental luxuries in 1592, swarmed with buyers and looters in pursuit of the vessel's rich cargo. From MS Cotton Augustus I, 1, f. 39; courtesy of the Trustees of the British Library.

54

The matter was delicate, for by order of his sovereign this courtier was currently confined in the Tower. Only a month before, the amazed and then wrathful Elizabeth had discovered that Ralegh had entered into a secret marriage with one of her ladies-in-waiting and was now the father of a son. Abruptly, her favorite was revealed as unfaithful to the exchange of platonic persiflage she had enjoyed for a decade. Her previous favorite, Robert Dudley, earl of Leicester, had similarly betrayed her. Their behavior was an outrage to a Virgin Queen.

But in financial matters Elizabeth was a Tudor. She ordered Ralegh to be brought out, under guard, and taken to Dartmouth. On his arrival, the fervor of the acclaim he received amazed Cecil; and though the pillage was far advanced, Ralegh retrieved a considerable amount of treasure from the snatchers.

In the final tally, the ship itself, many precious stones, and £141,200 were on hand to be divided. Of this Elizabeth took £80,000 and saw to it that the share allotted to Ralegh reflected her continuing displeasure. Ralegh and his brother Carew had planned the strategy for capturing the carrack. He had even volunteered and equipped his *Roebuck* for the chase, and for the expedition had advanced £34,000, of which £11,000 was borrowed at interest. For all of this, he received £36,000.

Hawkins estimated that the cargo of the *Madre de Diós*, when intact, had been worth £500,000. Before the looting began, the prize had on board 537 tons of spices, 8,500 hundredweight of pepper, 900 hundredweight of cloves, 700 hundredweight of cinnamon, 500 hundredweight of cochineal, 59 hundredweight of mace, 59 hundredweight of nutmeg, 50 hundredweight of benjamin, 15 tons of ebony, 2 great crosses and another large piece of jewelry studded with diamonds, and chests overflowing with musk, pearls, amber, calicoes, drugs, silks, ivory, tapestries, silver, and gold. With the possibility of occasional windfalls of such imposing dimensions, some members of ships' companies—those with an appreciation of skillful sailing, a stomach for a fight, and a stoical acceptance of the vagaries of fortune—voyaged with enthusiasm.

The individual characters and temperaments of the men at the upper levels in the chain of command stamped themselves on the outcome of any given voyage. A comparison of the experiences of colonists shipping under Sir Richard Grenville as captain-general in 1585 with those shipping under John White in 1587 is illustrative. Both captains-general had trouble with their associates, Grenville with governor-designate Ralph Lane and both Grenville and White with chief pilot Fernandes. But Grenville's training as a soldier gave him a power of command that secured his subordinates' compliance with his orders, while White the artist was overridden by Fernandes and his crew.

V. Varied Cargo

On all long voyages, English ships carried two kinds of cargo: supplies necessary to operate and repair the vessel and maintain those on board, and military equipment required by its complement of soldiers and gunners. Boatswains were quite familiar with stowing this cargo, although the average ship's limited storage spaces—two closed decks with a 3-foot clearance between them—required crewmen to exercise both ingenuity and practice. But ships carrying colonists also had to accommodate large additions to such cargo. Space had to be found for the colonists themselves and for everything they would need both during their trip and afterward, when survival demanded self-sufficiency. In 1584 a correspondent prepared "For Master Rawley's Viage" a list of the number and kinds of armed men he thought requisite to the 1585 colony's self-defense, and Richard Hakluyt's *Discourse Concerning Western Planting* lists the colony's requirements for self-maintenance.

The correspondent's military list envisaged far larger numbers than were placed in America for many years: 800 men, half of whom would be harquebusiers and the others swordsmen, longbowmen, and men armed with lesser weapons. All needed special equipment. Hakluyt warned that support of battle-ready troops required experts in the arts of fortification and makers of military supplies and equipment such as pikes and halberd staves, glue, arrows, spades to dig trenches, baskets to carry dirt, saltpeter and gunpowder, and shields and doublets.

Hakluyt's estimate of the colony's economic needs included consumable items to be brought over ready for use, as well as roots, vegetables, seasonings, and basic grains—"Wheat, Rye, Barley, Bigge, or Barley Beare, Oates, Beanes, Pease, Facchis, three square Graine, to sowe to vitell by breade and drinke, &c."—to be planted upon arrival. He recommended that live animals—hogs, rabbits, doves, chickens, ducks, and turkeys—be picked up at island stops near the end of the voyage and that it would also be wise to have "greyhounds to kill deere, &c, Mastives to kill heavy beastes of ravyne and for night watches, Bloudehoundes to recover hurte dere."

The skills he thought necessary to the new economy exceeded those available in all but a very few English centers: for mobility and for fishing, colonists should know how to build ships, pinnaces, and small boats and how to make such gear as oars, cable, and cordage. Since all equipment would have to be fashioned from raw materials, the shipbuilders must be backed by "grubbers and rooters upp of cipres, cedars, and all other faire trees," sawyers, coopers, blacksmiths, carpenters and joiners, pitch and tar makers, and millwrights to build sawmills and gristmills.

For raising and preparing food, there should be "sugar cane planters with the plantes," gardeners, grafters, grape and olive experts, salt makers, butchers, bakers, brewers, cooks, hunters and fowlers, fishermen, and "knytters of nets." Hakluyt was also concerned that the colony include men with skills needed to provide shelter and wearing apparel as well as for defense and livelihood—men who could use an adze and put on a weatherproof thatch, tan leather, tailor clothes, and make shoes.

If the new village were to flourish, each individual would clearly have to play many parts. The settlement would need a few substantial buildings sided with boards and many dwelling huts constructed of wattle and daub; all of these structures would require thatched roofs. A first consideration would be a water supply—either a running source and casks in which to catch it, or cask-lined wells. Since the Outer Banks consist of a single long sandbar, both clay to make fired bricks for cooking hearths and stone (or bricks) for chimneys would be scarce.

In the eyes of Ralegh's boatswains, those passengers who possessed such skills were just so much cargo, to be placed aboard and kept out of the way of the ship's operations. With more than a hundred planters in addition to each ship's crew and soldiers during the outbound trips, scarce space was squeezed almost beyond the limit.

Except for the colony's officers and perhaps a few others who were entitled to quarters in the sterncastle, most of the planters had to be quartered in the hold. They were allowed only sporadic access to light and air on the open deck when the weather was fair, the wind constant, and the sea gentle. During the 1587 voyage, everyone was allowed a breather of three days on shore after the expedition reached the West Indies. The event rated special mention in John White's log. "We came to anker at the Island called Santa Cruz," he wrote, "where all the planters were set on land, staying there till the 25 of the same month." Men and women accustomed on their home island to summer temperatures ranging around 65 degrees must have welcomed even a brief escape from closed quarters inside a small ship moving through a subtropical area in June and July.

Such were the various tangible cargoes that troubled the boatswains. The ships likewise carried intangible cargoes that troubled the captains-general. At the same time that experienced mariners proffered lists of useful commodities for colonizing enterprises, knowledgeable policy makers were furnishing for consideration by the adventurers and the queen lists of the purposes that such enterprises might serve. In relation to genuine possibilities, some of these purposes recalled the inaccuracies of early maps. The more readily feasible objectives were not necessarily attainable in combination with each other. The men who set sail for America carried with them a variety of expectations about which conflict was inevitable.

Until the mid-1570s, colonization had not been seriously suggested—privateering and the discovery of trade routes had been the objective of deep-sea voyaging. But though the queen was chary of challenging established Spanish settlements in the new hemisphere's central section, areas "not subject to any

Christian prince" lay open to the north and to the south of it. In the interest of claiming and settling these non-Christian lands, early English explorers began to solicit Elizabeth's attention.

A quick and unchallenged route to the riches of the Orient was still a dominant English desire; each of the new exploration projects, therefore, proposed the discovery of such a route as a primary purpose. Richard Grenville and Humphrey Gilbert almost simultaneously petitioned Elizabeth for letters patent. Grenville desired to attempt to reach China via the mythical "Strait of Anian" by first rounding the southern tip of South America and then sailing north to enter the strait off the western North American coast. Humphrey Gilbert petitioned the queen for permission to seek the strait by way of North America's Arctic reaches.

Grenville's plan to arrive at Cathay by way of the Pacific, abandoned when permission was revoked by the queen, coincided with Sir Francis Drake's ambition to sail in those waters. In 1573, when Drake was in the Gulf of Mexico lying in wait to ambush the Spanish mule trains that brought gold and silver treasure up the west coast of Peru and across the Isthmus of Panama to Nombre de Diós, his Indian guides showed him the Pacific from the top of a "great and goodly high Tree." Drake "besought Almighty God of his goodness to give him life and leave to sail in an English ship in that sea."

The mythical Strait of Anian, believed to run above North America and lead directly to the Orient, is shown on Petrus Apian's "Map of the World," ca. 1550. Reproduced from a facsimile in the Collections of the Library of Congress, Geography and Map Division.

At the time of Drake's return from this expedition, Grenville was completing the preparation of A *Discourse concerninge a Straighte to be discovered towarde the northweste passinge to Cathaia, and the Orientall Indians, withe a confutacion of their errour that thinke the discouerye thereof to be most conveniently attempted to the North of Baccalaos.* (Baccalaos was the name given to Newfoundland and Labrador.) As the title suggests, Grenville contrasted the northern and southern routes to Cathay and enumerated the advantages offered by the latter. He discounted two major objections to his proposal—the length of the journey and the tropical heat to be endured when crossing the equatorial zone on both sides of South America—by noting that English mariners were already familiar with the southern course as far down as the lower limits of Brazil; and he contrasted the heat of the southern route, relieved by cooler night temperatures, with the ceaseless cold and the dangers of ice and fog in the frozen Arctic. Because only Magellan had then rounded South America's southern tip, Grenville's prospectus could without contradiction "omytte the rages of the Seas and tempestuous wether" by which ships would be "farre more often andaungered in the *Northe* then in the *Southe*." And he assured the queen that he and his fellow applicants were prepared to meet the entire cost of the venture.

The document was exceptional in that it did not confine itself to discussing the search for access to the riches of the Orient. Colonization as well as exploration was an integral part of the plan. At a time when the mother country was held to be overpopulated, overseas settlement would put "Idle and nedie people to worke. . . . It is no dispeoplinge. The people abonde as apperethe by the nomber greter then can welbe provided for." With a settlement at the mouth of the River Plate, fortification of the Magellan Strait, and further settlements on the west coast of South America, England would be well placed among the New World's occupying forces.

On receipt of this petition, the queen exercised her frequently used right of vacillation. Initially she gave Grenville the requested letters patent, and he began preparations; but after he had acquired two or three ships and was negotiating for several others, she heard that there were Spanish settlements beyond the Strait of Magellan that might contest Grenville's presence. Quickly, she revoked the letters. Crushed with disappointment, the proud Grenville turned away from the sea and retired to private life for nearly a decade. The scene he ordered carved in the marble of the main overmantel in the house to which he converted the nave of the great church at Buckland Abbey is a chapter of autobiography. It displays a knight who has removed and set aside his armor and turned his warhorse loose. Sitting alone with a skull and an hourglass, the knight meditates on man's impermanence and the uncertainty of destiny.

In 1577, though Grenville would not learn of it until 1580, the irony of the queen's change of mind became bitterly evident. Drake's circumnavigation followed the exact course described in Grenville's *Discourse*: across to Brazil, south past the River Plate, through the Strait of Magellan, up South America's west coast past the isthmus where the "great and goodly high Tree" stood, and well along the North American shore before turning west (with no need for a "Strait of Anian") to the Spice Islands of the Orient and on round the remainder of the globe.

Simultaneously with Grenville's proposal, Humphrey Gilbert's *Discourse of a Discoverie for a new Passage to Cataia* also sought permission to plant a colony. His was to be located at the entrance of the passage he expected to find by sailing around the top of the western hemisphere. Gilbert received the

Sir Humphrey Gilbert, Ralegh's half brother, hoped to find a northwest passage to the Orient over North America and establish a colony near its eastern entrance; but his efforts failed, and he perished in a storm while returning to England in 1583. From Holland, *Herωologia Anglica* (1620), plate 64; by permission of the Folger Shakespeare Library.

queen's permission, but Grenville proved to have been right about the rigors of the northern climate and Gilbert did not even attempt to find a northwest passage.

Six years later, while awaiting return of the ships Ralegh had dispatched to explore the possibility of planting a colony on the middle Atlantic coast of North America, Richard Hakluyt, at Ralegh's request, wrote *A Discourse of Western Planting*. He called its twenty-three chapters "A brefe collection of certaine reasons to induce her Majestie and the state to take in hande the westerne voyage and the plantings there." His reasons, some of which repeat those of Gilbert, fall into three main categories: the special promise of an uncontested northern seaway, the economic gains to be realized from a plantation in the West, and the military advantage of locating a base on the new continent.

According to Hakluyt, the course to North America, since it did not cut across the trade routes of any foreign power, was a safe one; and it could be undertaken at any time of year, unlike either the much-used route to the Levant via Gibraltar, which was often becalmed in summer, or the passage above the Scandinavian countries to Russia, which was hampered for long periods by winter cold.

The colony, as it developed trade, would require merchant ships capable of moving large quantities of freight. For that reason, Hakluyt wrote, "this realme shall have by that means shippes of greate burden" and skilled sailors "which kinde of men are neither nourished in few daies nor in few years." Because of the distance from Europe, the new ships were not likely to be driven by storms into the ports of foreign princes, as Spanish ships were often driven into England's West Country ports. English merchants, therefore, would not suffer large cargo losses.

The colony would give occupation to "the frye of the wandringe beggars of England that grow upp idly" and would alleviate overcrowding in English trades. In addition, soldiers released from the army at the end of wars, who in the past had sometimes threatened "the quiete of this realme," could find honest work, and mariners laid off after relatively short trips to nearby coasts would have steadier employment over the longer course to North America. These men would neither take to piracy out of necessity nor be attracted to it by the "riche praye for them to take"—temptations then commonly experienced. And in the colony, some of the men with fertile minds and varied gifts, whom youthful follies had forced to leave England to avoid the gallows, could return to useful lives.

Hakluyt claimed that because "The soyle yeldeth, and may be made to yelde, all the severall commodities of Europe," the employment available to immigrants would be varied: men were needed to cut the excellent trees for timber and masts with which to build ships and to supply them with pitch and tar; workers could exploit salt pans; and by planting vines and olives, citrus fruit and figs, as well as carrying on more familiar types of husbandry, colonists could foster so much new trade that "we shall cutt the combe of the Frenche, of the Spanish, of the Portingal."

While English traffic in wool and cloth had historically been the source of a steady rise in English wealth, in recent years it had been menaced by increased Spanish wool-growing at home and in the West Indies. Establishment of a New World trade would provide many markets to serve settlers in the northern parts of America, "to whom warme clothe shalbe righte welcome," and to inhabitants of as yet unvisited islands and dominions.

"Whereas now the realme becomes the poorer by the purchasinge of forreine commodities in so great a masse at so excessive prices," products from a colony would be available to the English market free from the multiple tariffs and customs fees currently imposed on them en route. Merchants with factors in the New World could repair and load their cargoes without marking their prices up to cover foreign harbor charges. By being able to trade with smaller stocks, they would be relieved of borrowing to finance extensive supplies and consequently could sell at lower prices in England. Also, because North America contained known deposits of iron, "wee may oute of those partes receive the masse of wrought wares that now we receave out of Fraunce, Flaunders, Germanye, &c."

The economic advantages of a colony were central among Hakluyt's reasons for planting, but military/political purposes were important too:

This enterprise may staye the Spanish Kinge from flowinge over all the face of that waste firme of America, yf wee by plantinge there in time, in tyme I say . . . shall lett him from makinge more shorte and more safe returnes. . . . The Spaniardes governe in the Indies with all pride and tyranie . . . so no doubte whensoever the Queene of England, a prince of such clemencie shall seate upon that firme of America . . . they will yield themselves to her government, and revolte cleane from the Spaniards . . . and this broghte so aboute, her Majestie and her subjectes may bothe enjoye the treasure of the mynes of golde and silver, and the whole trade and all the gaine of the trade of marchandize, that nowe passeth thither by the Spaniards onely hands. . . . The English can become lordes of all those sees . . . and consequently to abate the pride of Spaine and of the supporter of the great Antechriste of Rome. . . .

The religious reference recalls that ever since Martin Luther's time, England and Spain, in contesting territory, had been mindful of the European balance between countries whose sovereigns were determinedly loyal to the Church of Rome and those in which various reformed or separated churches had broken with Rome and received national political recognition. English colonies would add weight to the Protestant side of this uneasy balance: "Wee shall by plantinge there inlarge the glory of the gospell, and from Englande plante sincere religion, and provide a safe and a sure place to receave people from all partes of the worlde that are forced to flee for the truthe of Gods worde," Hakluyt declared.

If the reasons for planting a colony were broad and varied, so too were the temperaments and motivations of the Englishmen who undertook the expedition. Correspondence and diaries of those who traveled aboard the *Tiger* in the Roanoke expedition of 1585 report the quarrels that surfaced as Grenville, Lane, Fernandes, and their respective supporters disagreed with each other. These men had different natures and backgrounds. Grenville's courage, as shown in his final, fatal sea battle in the *Revenge* in 1591, was matched by his pride. Lane's military experience during the atrocities in Ireland, from which he had been withdrawn to receive his Virginia governorship, had made him ill prepared for civil administration and still less for coexistence with native tribes. Fernandes's immediate past record as chief pilot on Edward Fenton's expedition had shown him to be a knowledgeable deep-sea navigator but also a braggart and a willful man. Inevitably, their personalities rasped on each other.

In the "Preface to the Gentle Reader" of his *Briefe and True Report*, Harriot analyzed the divisive friction that began on shipboard among the ill-sorted members of Ralegh's first colony:

> Of our companie that returned some for their misdemeanour and ill dealing in the countrey, have been there worthily punished; who by reason of their bad natures, haue maliciously not onelie spoken ill of their Gouernour but for their sakes slaundered the countrie itself . . . many that after golde and siluer was not so soone found, as it was by them looked for, had little or no care of any other thing but to pamper their bellies. . . . Some also were of nice bringing vp. . . . Because there were not to be found any English cities, nor such faire houses, nor at their owne wish any of their olde accustomed daintie food, nor any soft beds of downe or fethers; the country was to them miserable. . . .

The expedition's courageous travelers sought varied objectives in establishing a colony. For those with short-term interest in quick gain, a colony on the American mainland would serve chiefly as a naval base from which to pursue the great carracks that bore Spanish riches home. And, lest local riches be overlooked, some of the get-rich-quick-minded settlers, upon landing, scattered to search for metal mines (preferably with gold-bearing seams) rather than engaging in the immediate business of planting crops and putting up houses. A large part of the support given to the Ralegh voyage from the most eminent sources—his own, the queen's, those of highly placed courtiers and ministers of state—was speculative money advanced with rapid yields in view.

Others had different ends in mind. Most of the West Country families, from whom came the great sea captains, had over the past century risen higher in the gentry class by the acquisition of land. Many colonizing families believed that they could achieve similar status by beginning with the 500 acres guaranteed to every New World planter. Some of the men with this expectation were backed by money for the Ralegh voyages that came from merchants in London and elsewhere who expected the expedition to become a long-term investment.

Although Harriot knew that personality differences and varying motivations among colonists might cause problems, his own experience had convinced him that under serious planters a permanent colony could succeed:

> I will make declaration of such commodities there alreaddie found or to be raised, which will not onely serue the ordinary turnes of you which are and shall bee of the planters and inhabitants, but such an ouerplus . . . as by way of trafficke and exchaunge with our owne nation of England, will enrich your selues the prouiders; those that shal deal with you; the enterpreisers in general; and greatly profit our owne countrey men, to supply them with most things which heretofore they have been faine to prouide, either of strangers or of our enemies.

The cargo of expectations carried aboard Ralegh's little ships was volatile stuff. Conflicting desires among groups as diverse as planters and privateers were bound to cause some eyes to scan the horizon for landfall, others for a sail. Ralegh's ventures foundered in the crosscurrents created by their multiple purposes.

VI. The First Colony's Crossing

By the 1580s, Spain and England were nearing the end of a political chess match for which both Europe and America were the chessboard. At the zenith of his power, Philip II of Spain anticipated that his next move would be the winning checkmate.

By conquering and occupying Protestant England, the Spanish king hoped to avenge Elizabeth's imprisonment of Catholic Mary, Queen of Scots; to surround his Continental rival, France, with territories subject to the Holy Roman Empire; and to end all challenge to the pope's division of the New World. In the Western Hemisphere, Philip's hold was firm from Mexico to Peru. On the Florida peninsula, his forces had wiped out the French Huguenots' colony of the 1560s and reestablished Spanish power at Saint Augustine. In the 1570s Spanish voyages of reconnaissance had explored the Atlantic Coast as far up as Chesapeake Bay, where a Jesuit mission maintained a foothold for some months before it was destroyed by Indians.

In 1585 England and Spain broke diplomatic relations. England made a double thrust into the New World during that year when two related expeditions sailed, one initiated by Sir Walter Ralegh in April and one captained by Sir Francis Drake in September. Drake's commission was to make a series of sudden strikes—at Santiago in Spain's Cape Verde Islands, at Santo Domingo in the West Indies, at Cartagena on the South American coast of the Gulf of Mexico, and at Saint Augustine in Florida. His awe-inspiring fleet numbered twenty-three ships, and he had Martin Frobisher as his vice-admiral and Richard Hawkins as one of his captains. Ralegh's venture was to plant inside North Carolina's Outer Banks a permanent English settlement that could support the queen's navy in close proximity to the area where its strength was likely to be needed. The French had proved that locations farther south attracted immediate Spanish retaliation, and a site much farther north would have been too far away to be useful.

The fort built at Puerto Rico's Mosquito Bay by Ralegh's captain-general, Sir Richard Grenville, during his outbound voyage in 1585 was in clear anticipation of military action. In the game of international chess, Ralegh's move to establish a colony was equivalent to the advancing of a pawn. When the pawn's position proved untenable, Drake's fleet sacrificed it and removed the settlers before the Spaniards could act.

Ralegh began to assemble a fleet of men and ships in September, 1584, following the return of two young members of his household, Philip Amadas of Plymouth and Arthur Barlowe, whom he had sent out in April under Fernandes's pilotage to examine the North American coast between Florida and Norumbega (New England). They brought Ralegh an assessment of the

Sir Richard Grenville, captain-general of Ralegh's 1585 expedition to Roanoke Island. National Portrait Gallery, London.

recommended site at Roanoke Island, a description of its appearance, and two Indians—Wanchese and Manteo.

Ralegh presented the Indians at court and gave the queen Hakluyt's *Discourse of Western Planting*. Elizabeth ordered her own ship *Tiger* to serve as the expedition's flagship. She also contributed 400 pounds of gunpowder from the royal stores. Her support of the project enticed several courtiers to advance funds. By spring, 1585, a seven-vessel squadron was ready.

The flagship of the fleet was the *Tiger*, rebuilt in various years and variously rated at 120, 140, 160, and 200 tons, probably 200 tons at this date. She carried both Sir Richard Grenville, captain-general and admiral, and Ralph Lane, a gentleman from Lympstone on Devon's River Exe, one of the queen's equerries and recently with her forces in Ireland; he was the ship's lieutenant and the colony's governor-designate. Francis Brooke, gentleman, privateer, and treasurer of the colony, also had a berth.

Simon Fernandes was master of the *Tiger* and chief pilot of the fleet. The two men commissioned to record the appearance and the resources of mid-America, Thomas Harriot and John White, were aboard, as were the Indians Manteo and Wanchese.

Next in the squadron was the *Roebuck*, Ralegh's own flyboat, named for the deer that topped the crest of his coat of arms. The 140-ton vessel, captained by John Clarke, had Philip Amadas, admiral-designate of Virginia, on board. Other vessels included the *Lion*, later called *Red Lion*, 100 tons, captained by George Raymond, and the *Elizabeth*, 50 tons, owned and captained by Thomas Cavendish, high marshall (chief judicial officer) of the fleet. (Ralegh's pinnace *Dorothie*, 50 tons, is listed as starting but is not mentioned later in the voyage.) There were two other pinnaces, one of which was the *Tiger*'s tender.

On April 9, in the prime sailing season, the expedition was gaily waved out of Plymouth harbor, with Mayor Christopher Brooking acclaiming in his minute book that "Sir Richard Grendefelde, knight, departed from Plymouth wth vi shippes and barkes for Wingane Dehoy where he carried vi. hundred men or thereabouts." But as the ships headed south toward the Canaries, their orderly progress was broken by a violent storm in the Bay of Portugal. The *Tiger*'s pinnace was sunk and the fleet did not reassemble, though the other ships, with perhaps the exception of the *Dorothie*, reached Roanoke at one time or another. Thanks to the diligent Richard Hakluyt, the course of the flagship is known in detail.

On April 14, after a stop at the Canaries, the *Tiger* sailed westward and was rewarded with a quick passage to the West Indies. At the end of the first week of May, the ship's company sniffed the sweet smell of landfall that Arthur Barlowe had extolled in his account of the expedition of the previous year. "We found shole water," he wrote, "wher we smelt so sweet, and so strong a smel, as if we had bene in the midst of some delicate garden abounding with all kinde of odoriferous flowers, by which we were assured, that the land could not be farre distant."

Shortly afterward, they sighted Dominica. (White's first watercolor of the

The flagship of the 1585 expedition to Roanoke Island was Elizabeth's own *Tiger*, loaned for the voyage. The National Maritime Museum, London.

voyage was a profile of "Markes" of the island.) But Grenville did not stop there. Instead, he coasted along the south side of Puerto Rico to the little island of Cotesa, where the shipbound travelers enjoyed a day's rest ashore.

While in the islands, members of the ship's company who had never been in subtropical climates became acquainted not only with a new landscape but also with unfamiliar flora and fauna. White, who had been drawing the flying fish that gleamed with phosphorus as they broke water beside the ship's bow in the evening, now drew a comparable land insect, "a flye which in the night semeth a flame of fyer." They saw iguanas and alligators. Among edible fruits, they enjoyed mammee apples, pineapples, and bananas and brought sugar cane and banana plants aboard to plant later.

The *Tiger*'s journal does not mention illness resulting from experimental eating of unknown fruits, but the record of the 1587 voyage reports that on a stop at Santa Cruz, "some of our women, and men, by eating a small fruit like greene Apples were fearefully troubled with a sudden burning in their mouthes, and swelling of their tongues so bigge, that some of them could not speake. Also a child by sucking one of those women's breasts, had at that instant his mouth set on such a burning, that it was strange to see how the infant was tormented for the time; but after 24 houres, it ware away of it selfe." Nor is there any mention of onslaughts by the voracious salt-marsh mosquito, though the ship's next stop was at Puerto Rico's Mosquito (Guayanilla) Bay.

There, anchoring the *Tiger* offshore, the company landed and began work on two substantial projects. One was to replace the pinnace lost off Portugal; the other, to build a fort. From the felling of the necessary trees to the completed

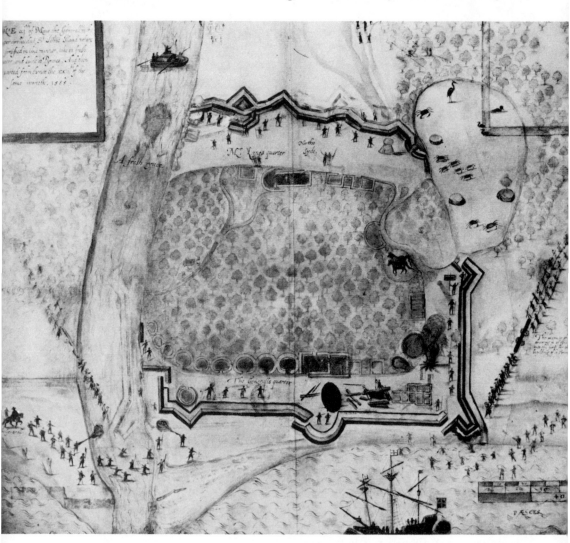

The 1585 expedition to Roanoke Island stopped en route at Puerto Rico's Mosquito (Guayanilla) Bay. John White's watercolor shows the fort that the company constructed there, with the ship *Tiger* in the foreground. Reproduced from the Page-Holgate facsimiles of the American Drawings of John White, the North Carolina Collection of the Wilson Library of the University of North Carolina at Chapel Hill, by permission of the University of North Carolina Press.

boat, the pinnace was finished in ten days.

An illuminating drawing by John White shows both works in progress. The fort is laid off at the edge of the shore, using a freshwater river as one of its side boundaries. Inside the enclosure, men are working on the pinnace; a fire, probably for forging iron, is visible nearby. Shown approaching the fort from the right are men with ropes pulling in a large tree to supply the shipwrights with additional lumber; they are followed by a number of guards. On the left, Grenville on horseback and a contingent of soldiers are returning along the shore, perhaps from a parley concerning the purchase of supplies. Two captured horses are in a corral within the fort. At the water's edge, close to the pinnace builders, a sconce protects an opening to the sea through which the new boat will be launched. The *Tiger* rides in the foreground, in deep water.

As work went forward, Grenville received a very pleasant surprise. On May 19, 1585, a sail on the horizon, at first taken to be that of a Spanish vessel, turned out to be Captain Cavendish in the *Elizabeth*; his arrival very considerably raised Grenville's numbers. Grenville had good reason to welcome the additions, for at the island's capital of San Juan, the Spanish governor had been informed of the coming of the English. He instructed his lieutenant at San German, the town at the island's southwest corner, to take a force of forty and observe the new arrivals.

As soon as the soldiers arrived, Grenville sent a party to propose amicable trade with the Spanish and arranged for an additional rendezvous two days later. When the rendezvous was not kept, however, he became suspicious and departed after setting fire to the surrounding woods, dismantling parts of the fort, and leaving on a post the information that the *Tiger* and the *Elizabeth* had been there in case other English ships should call. Grenville departed in advance of thirty-five Spanish harquebusiers whom the governor had sent to hold the English in their fort. At the west end of the island, in the Mona Channel, he captured a small Spanish frigate that turned out to be empty and then a larger one loaded with cloth and other consumer goods for the Spanish settlements.

To increase the expedition's supply of salt, Grenville then ordered Lieutenant Ralph Lane to take twenty men in the small captured frigate and raid the salt pans in Rojo Bay at Puerto Rico's southwest tip. After mustering a larger number of men, Lane landed and found two piles of salt ready for removal. He had started to load the salt when he was surprised by the sudden arrival of armed Spaniards. In alarm, he jumped to the conclusion that they were a full-scale force led by the governor. (In fact, they seem to have been only the San German garrison, and they did no more than observe.) Lane loaded the remaining salt and sailed away. Nothing untoward had happened, but the incident gave rise to one of the serious quarrels between captain-general and governor-designate and between captain-general and chief pilot, with Lane an active partisan of Fernandes. Lane insisted that Grenville had wrongfully and recklessly exposed him to mortal danger. Writing Sir Francis Walsingham from Roanoke, Lane complained bitterly; and in reminiscences he set down seven years later he exaggerated further.

My exceptione vnto him for . . . his engaginge of me with my onely squadre of xxv. Souldiours and sixe Spanishe prisoners, with mattockes, and Spades, (at Cape Rosso against the governour there Diego Melindes with fortye horse & -300- foote) to lade salte, where he toulde me I shoulde fynde none to resiste, but findinge the contrary, my tellinge him of it bred the grete vnkindness afterwardes one his parte towardes me.

White's map of the fort at Guayanilla Bay symbolizes the distance that animosity put between Lane and Grenville: the quarters of the two men are indicated at opposite corners of the enclosure.

While Lane was loading salt, Grenville, with the *Tiger*, the *Elizabeth*, the larger of the two captured Spanish frigates, and the new pinnace, engaged in successful trade along Puerto Rico's southern coast. As Hawkins had discovered during his slaving voyages twenty years earlier, the desire for consumer goods was apt to outweigh political loyalties in those parts, and illegal trade under French as well as Spanish auspices flourished there. Grenville could elicit little interest among the traders in ransoming the prisoners he had

Sir Thomas Cavendish commanded his own ship *Elizabeth* on Ralegh's first colonizing venture in 1585 and a year later became the second Englishman to circumnavigate the globe. Holland, *Herwologia Anglica* (1620), facing p. 88; by permission of the Folger Shakespeare Library.

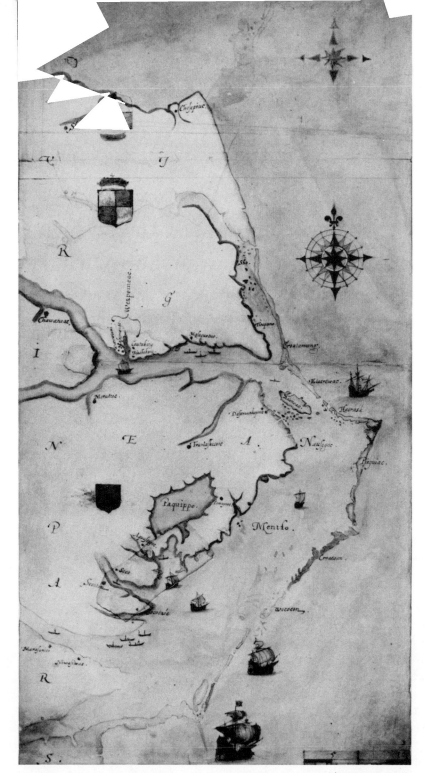

The American coastal area from Chesapeake Bay southward to Cape Lookout; Roanoke Island, site of the first English colony, is located about midway. Ralegh stipulated that his second colony (1587) should be established on the southern shore of Chesapeake Bay, but his chief pilot refused to take the settlers beyond Roanoke. Reproduced from the Page-Holgate facsimiles by permission of the University of North Carolina Press.

captured in the Spanish frigates, but bidding was brisk for the cloth and other goods from his second prize. The *Tiger*'s shipboard life was enlivened by livestock purchased for the colony—hogs, cattle, and horses.

On May 29 the five-vessel fleet turned toward the north coast of Hispaniola, stopping at Puerto de Plata and anchoring in Isabela harbor for two days of transactions with French illegal traders. The town governor and the warden of the Puerto de Plata fort proved friendly; on June 5 Grenville and his officers were invited ashore for a feast, a bullfight, and sports. The following day they acquired more horses (these with saddles and bridles), cattle, sheep, swine, and plants, and, with thoughts of the home market, some hides, sugar, ginger, pearls, and—most precious of all—tobacco.

On June 7 the expedition went on its way, stopping at an island of seals—where the ships were close to being lost—then searching in vain for more salt on one of the Caicos Islands. On the north side of the Bahamas, they touched on Eleuthera, with another landing on Great Abaco. On the twentieth, as they moved through Providence North Channel, they had their first sighting of the American mainland, but they did not go ashore.

Carefully, they worked their way up the coast. On the twenty-third they ran into shoals, probably off Cape Fear, and anchored the following day to fish. From Cape Fear they followed the Outer Banks as far north as an inlet called Wococon, probably near the middle of present-day Portsmouth Island. There, instead of continuing to the inlet at the north end of Hatteras Island—named Port Ferdinando in honor of Fernandes by the reconnaissance expedition the year before—the pilot, leaving the *Tiger* anchored offshore, attempted entry into Pamlico Sound with the other boats. All grated aground. According to Lane, the entry at Port Ferdinando had a depth of 12 feet at high tide; the Wococon bar was very shallow. It was more by good luck than good management that the grounded boats were floated off on the next high tide.

The following day, in spite of this experience, Fernandes attempted to bring the *Tiger* over. Predictably, she ploughed into the sand and for two solid hours lay in the surf, pounded by every incoming crest. The crew, estimating that she received some eighty-nine buffets, was sure that her back would be broken. Yet, when she was finally freed and beached, she proved to be sturdy; her back was not broken, and she sailed again after being repaired.

Nevertheless, the grounding caused an irrecoverable catastrophe. As the largest ship in the fleet, and with the 50-ton *Elizabeth* the only other of those leaving Plymouth as yet accounted for, the *Tiger* contained supplies that comprised the colony's sustenance for the coming winter. The planters would have to rely on these foodstuffs until arrival of a relief ship or the ripening of the next harvest. But the stranding had rendered most provisions unusable; the entire cargo was soaked in salt water.

In the following days, the bleakness of the expedition's predicament brightened only slightly—and the supply situation not at all—with news that two more of the original fleet had apparently completed their journey. After a storm-harassed crossing, during which he had been forced to abandon a number of his men on Jamaica for lack of food, Captain George Raymond in the *Lion* had reached Croatoan Island to the north of Wococon in mid-June. There he had deposited some thirty colonists, two of whom were found later by Grenville's men, and sailed for home via Newfoundland. That Captain John Clarke in the *Roebuck* arrived is known only because his name appears as a member of the group that accompanied Grenville's exploration of Pamlico Sound in mid-July. On July 21 the fleet moved to Hatteras, where on the twenty-ninth, Grangani-meo, brother of Chief Wingina, with Manteo as interpreter, arrived to discuss the location of the colony's fort and town. The selected site on Roanoke Island held more promise for permanent settlement than for privateering. Sheltered behind the Outer Banks, the location was unlikely to attract Spanish attention. But the absence of a harbor of any depth nullified its usefulness as a center of supply and repair for warlike expeditions such as that which Drake was then assembling.

A decision had, however, been made. On August 5 John Arundell, a member of the company, was dispatched to England to inform Ralegh and the queen of the completion of the voyage and to urge quick replacement of the *Tiger's* waterlogged cargo.

On the twenty-fifth, Grenville started home. Within a week he captured a 300-ton Spanish ship, the *Santa Maria de San Vicente*, carrying an excellent cargo. He must have left his longboat behind for the colony's use, because the record of the capture reveals that he boarded the Spanish vessel by using "a boate made with boards of chests, which fell a sunder, and sunke at the shippes side, assoone as euer hee and his men were out of it." Grenville remained aboard the slower-moving prize, and a storm separated her from the *Tiger*.

The *Tiger* reached Falmouth on October 6, 1585. When the captain-general and his prize arrived at Plymouth on the eighteenth, there to be "courteiously received by divers of his worshipfull friends," Ralegh was awaiting him. Sale of the *San Vicente*, ship and cargo, brought £50,000. That amount covered the entire cost of the expedition and gave adventurers in the colony a dividend of £10,000. Supplies were needed at Roanoke, but prospects for the settlement were bright.

VII. The Unreached Destination

By mid-1586 the bright prospects of the Roanoke colony had darkened into gloom. On July 28 Drake's fleet entered Portsmouth harbor, and one by one the surviving members of Ralegh's first settlement disembarked. Voyaging home from the Caribbean, Drake had called to see how the Roanoke planters fared and, finding them in dire condition, brought them home.

On leaving them the previous year, Grenville had promised that he would be back with supplies before Easter; it was summer when he returned to Roanoke. Delays in preparations had kept him in England, and his return was further postponed when his supply vessel ran aground on the shallow Bideford Bar in Bideford Bay. In the nearby town of Barnstaple, the town clerk noted the accident in his diary: "16. April afore[sd] Richard Greynvylle sailed over the bar with his flee boat and frigat but for want of suffic[t] water on the barr being neare upon neape he left his ship. This Sir Richard Greynvylle pretended his goinge to Wynganecora where he was last year." As the result of Grenville's difficulties, the Roanoke colony was without assistance from England until Drake's fleet sighted the settlement on June 9, 1586.

Drake first made Lane a gratefully accepted offer of supplies and a good-sized ship to give the settlers mobility. But as the supplies and ship were being transferred, a great storm wrecked the proffered vessel and forced the rest of Drake's fleet to stand well offshore. Demoralized by the destruction, the colonists begged Drake to take them with him; when he agreed, they tumbled their gear into the longboats in such a hurry that many articles, including all of Harriot's notes and some of White's drawings, were allowed to fall overboard. By nightfall on June 19 the site at Roanoke was vacant.

A minuscule difference in the timing of the arrival of supplies could have prevented the colony's departure. Only days after Drake left for England, a lone sail topped the horizon: at his own expense, Ralegh had dispatched a supply ship in advance of the Grenville fleet. The captain of Ralegh's vessel searched the island and departed. Within two weeks after the departure of Ralegh's relief attempt, Grenville's three ships arrived at Roanoke. Leaving fifteen or eighteen men to maintain the English claim to the area, Grenville too went home.

Ralegh braced to the bad news and in 1587 made a second effort. He converted his previously private venture into a company: on January 7, 1587, he was issued a charter instituting the Citie of Ralegh, to be run by a governor and twelve assistants. John White was named both governor and captain-general for the voyage. Once more, Simon Fernandes was chief pilot; he was also listed as an assistant.

The number of colonists transported (117) was slightly larger than in 1585,

Habes Lector candide fortiß ac inuictiß Ducis Draeck ad viuum Imaginem qui
toto terrarum orbe, duorum annorum, et mensium decem spatio, Zephiris fauen:
tibus circumducto, Anglium sedes proprias, 4. Cal Octobr: anno á partu Virgi:
nis 1580 reuisit cum antea portu soluisset sd. Decem: anni 1577.

Sir Francis Drake. National Portrait Gallery, London.

and this time there were women and children among them. The women included
John White's daughter Eleanor, who was the wife of Ananias Dare, one of the
assistants. The second expedition, however, was on a much more modest scale;
the ship *Lion* had only a flyboat and a pinnace for company.

Because most of the colonists on both expeditions bore names frequently found in England, attempts to trace them are plagued by ambiguities. Yet, from available data the identity of a number of individuals is clear, though that of others is conjectural. Meaningful comparison of the two groups is impossible: few of the 1587 contingent are known beyond their names on White's list, and except for records of university attendance, much of the identifying material for the 1585 planters concerns what they did later in life following their return to England. The colonists who composed both settlements at Roanoke were young.

In 1585, in addition to the captain-general and his brother-in-law, John Stukeley, a number of the company were listed as "Gentlemen." Cavendish, who began his circumnavigation a year later, and Abraham Kendall, a renowned mathematician and veteran navigator who had been one of Martin Frobisher's commanders in 1578, had a common interest in navigation. The expedition's treasurer, Francis Brooke, and two others also shared an interest: all three were "captains and promoters of privateering." Three men among the 1585 colonists had been in Parliament. One of the three, later sheriff of Cornwall, was one of Drake's executors. On the accession of King James I in 1603, three of the 1585 company were knighted.

Oxford and Cambridge were well represented on the first voyage: two men had been at Cambridge, seven at Oxford. On the second, there was one Cambridge man and a barrister with a degree from Oxford. One planter on the second voyage had been sheriff of Huntington; another, a muster captain of militia in 1582; and still another was on a 1585 militia muster roll.

A fairly wide range of skills, both in crafts and in husbandry, has been identified among the humbler voyagers of both expeditions. The 1587 list includes Jacob Whiddon, one of Ralegh's captains. Two of the 1587 settlers had previously been in jail, together, for stealing; one of those on the 1585 voyage apparently was later jailed for robbery. Judging from these fragments of evidence, the balance of intent of those on board seems to have tilted in 1585 toward privateering, and in 1587 toward permanency of settlement.

Ralegh's instructions to the new expedition were explicit: the second colony was not to settle at Roanoke Island. Repeated accidents resulting from the shallow bars at the inlets of the Outer Banks and the absence of any harbor that large ships could safely enter had proved the unsuitability of Roanoke Island as a location. An initial stop was to be made there to install the Indian Manteo as lord of the area and to collect any survivors of the detachment left by Grenville. But the destination of the voyage was to be Chesapeake Bay.

Ralph Lane, reporting on his governorship of the first colony, had told Ralegh of exploring north from Roanoke and finding

the Territorie and soyle of the Chesepians (being distant fifteene miles from the shoare) was for pleasantnes of seate, for temperature of Climate, for fertilitie of soyle, and for the commoditie of the Sea, besides multitude of beares (being an excellent good victual, with great woods of Sassafras, and Wall nut trees) is not to be excelled by any other whatsoeuer.

And Hakluyt, writing to Ralegh from Paris at the end of December, 1586, had strongly advised planting the new colony at Chesapeake Bay:

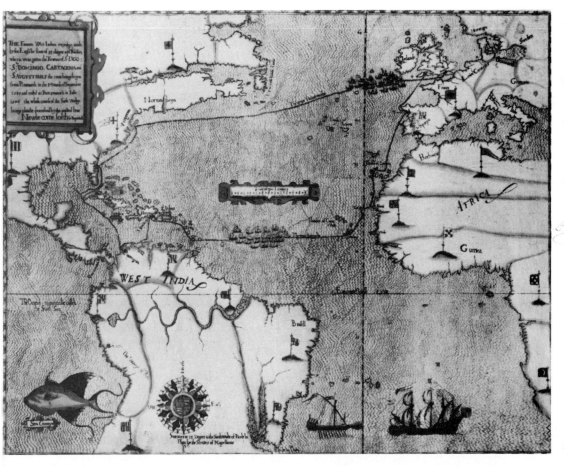

Battista Boazio's engraving traces the entire route of Sir Francis Drake's twenty-three-ship fleet in the 1585-1586 voyage at the end of which he brought the Roanoke settlers home. John Carter Brown Library, Brown University.

Yf you proceed, *which* I longe much to know, in yo*ur* enterprise of Virginia, your best planting wilbe aboute the bay of the Chesepians, to *whi*ch latitude Peter Martyr, and franciscus lopez de Gomara the Spaniard confesse that our Gabot and the English did first discover: *whi*ch the Spaniard*es* here after cannot deny us whensoever wee shalbe at Peace with them.

But the Ralegh expedition was not taken from Roanoke to Chesapeake Bay. Once at anchor at Roanoke, Simon Fernandes, whose faulty seamanship had deprived the first colony of its supplies, refused to take its successor to the site Ralegh had specified. When the ships made this first stop on July 22, 1587, after a crossing not materially different from its predecessor, the chief pilot insisted that the season was too far gone for further sailing. The falsity of his excuse became apparent when he did not depart for home for another month: the distance from Roanoke to Chespeake Bay was no more than a day's sail.

Governor White described the circumstances of Fernandes's refusal. On arrival near Roanoke Island,

The Gouernour went aboord the pinnesse, accompanied with fortie of his best men, intending to passe vp to Roanoake foorthwith, hoping there to finde those fifteen Englishmen, which Sir Richard Greenuill had left there the yeere before, with whome he meant to haue conference, concerning the state of the Countrey, and Sauages, meaning after he had so done, to returne againe to the fleete, and passe along the coast, to the Baye of Chesepiok, where we intended to make our seate and forte, according to the charge giuen us among other directions in writing, vnder the hande of Sir Walter Ralegh; but assoone as we were put with our pinnesse from the shippe, a Gentleman by the meanes of Fernando . . . called to the sailers in the pinnesse, charging them not to bring any of the planters backe againe, but leaue them in the Island, except the Gouernour, and two or three such as he approoued, saying that the Summer was farre spent, wherefore hee would land all the planters in no other place. Vnto this were all the sailers, both in the pinnesse, and shippe, perswaded by the Master, wherefore it booted not the Gouernour to contend with them.

Whether some of the colonists later completed the course to Chesapeake Bay is unknown. At the end of August, the planters insisted that White leave Roanoke and go to England for more settlers and more supplies. Until they put their case in the form of a letter to the queen, he refused, declaring that his enemies

would not spare to slander falsely both him and the action, by saying, hee went to Virginia, but politikely, and to no other end but to leade so many into a countrey, in which hee never meant to stay himselfe, and there to leave them behind him. Also he alleaged, that seeing they intended to remove 50 miles further up into the maine presently, he being then absent, his stuffe and goods might be both spoiled, & most of them pilfered away in the cariage. . . .

When White finally agreed to go, both he and the colonists who remained behind anticipated his prompt return.

But when White reached home, Philip of Spain was on the verge of sending the greatest fleet the world had yet seen into a definitive naval battle with the English, after which he expected to rule Elizabeth's realm. To meet this mortal threat, all English shipping was mobilized. Dispatch of relief to Ralegh's second colony was impossible. When White finally returned to Roanoke in 1590, he found an empty, disheveled, and deserted place, and his captain was unwilling to look further.

Ralegh fared still worse in 1602 when, partly because of renewal of interest in mid-American colonization, he sent one Captain Samuel Mace to attempt to locate the lost colonists. Historian William Strachey, in his *Historie of Travell into Virginia Britania*, says the trip was undertaken "if so be it they could happily light vpon them were like enough to enstruct vs the more perfectly, in the qualities of the Natives and Condicion of the the approved Country"; but the captain and crew, who

according to their Chardge should have sought the people both in the Islandes and vpon the Mayne in dyvers appointed places, they did yt not, pretending that the extreamity of weather and losse of some principall grownd-Tacklinge, forced and feared them from searching the Port of Hatarask, the Isle of Croatan, or any parte of the Mayne. . . . they returned, and brought no Comfort or new accesse of hope concerning the lives and saffety of the vnfortunate english people.

Each of the enterprises that Ralegh and Drake undertook in 1585 was regarded with a degree of disappointment in England. In the nation at large

The extent of Spain's empire in the New World, as displayed in a detail from an anonymous chart attributed to the period 1553-1563. Bild-Archiv der Oesterreichischen Nationalbibliothek, Vienna.

there was popular rejoicing that Drake had "singed the King of Spain's beard" by attacking Spanish holdings. But while Drake had captured important pieces of ordnance and other military equipment—he estimated the value of the loot his twenty-three ships brought back to England at not less than £50,000—he, unlike Grenville, had not boarded an expense-covering carrack laden with silver or Oriental luxuries. Consequently, the cost-conscious Privy Council rated his actions as without "so good successe as was hoped for." By 1590 stark failure had turned Ralegh's grant into vacant land, and White's unsuccessful search had written an end to England's first effort to establish a colony in the New World.

But there is a Spanish record, too, and it gives evidence that, measured in terms of resulting changes in Spain's policies, the two expeditions had been well worth England's while. Drake's Caribbean raids had terrified the Spanish; and during the ensuing years they continued to be frightened by fragmentary dispatches suggesting that the English might in fact have succeeded in establishing a settlement on or below Chesapeake Bay. These nagging intimations compelled Seville to acknowledge Drake's raids as proof that Spain's New World empire required better protection.

Grenville's observed presence in the West Indies in 1585, and especially his purchases of livestock (which could only have been in preparation for a nearby settlement), awakened vivid apprehensions among Spanish Caribbean governors. A dispatch to the king of Spain from Jamaica in June, 1586, confirmed Captain Raymond's forced landing there in the *Lion* during the previous year; two survivors from the group of men Raymond left behind had been found and questioned by the Spanish that September. Their depositions indicated that some six to eight years earlier, Fernandes had explored the Florida coast. (In the Spanish documents, the eastern coast as far up as the Spaniards' northernmost explorations is called Florida; included is the area in which "a great bay leads to where certain islands lie, and this is sweet water four leagues out to sea; and according to the Indians this is the best part of all the coast, and is a passage to the Pacific.")

In a series of reconnaissance expeditions, the Spanish paid special attention to this bay, which they called by varied names—sometimes Santa Maria de Jacán, sometimes Madre de Diós, and sometimes merely Jacán. On March 22, 1587, the president of the Havana House of Trade was informed that the governor of Florida believed that

150 leagues beyond Santa Elena [a Spanish settlement near today's Charleston], in Jacan, there is a settlement of English. . . . I am certain that the enemy has established a settlement there because it is so suitable a position from which to sally upon these Indies whenever they may desire, for they say they are settled directly west of Bermuda and so, because this would make them such close neighbours, I am as worried as though I knew certainly that they are there.

In June the Spanish governor, who had explored the North American coast as far as Chesapeake Bay in the early 1570s, was ordered to "discover whether any corsairs have settled in that coast." Leaving reinforcements at Santa Elena, he went up to the bay but failed to find English settlers.

In June, 1588, another search party entered Pamlico Sound, presumably at

Port Ferdinando. Working north, the party came upon "signs of a shipway for small vessels, and on land a number of wells made with English casks, and other debris indicating that a considerable number of people had been here"—how recently, the report does not say.

Also in 1588, a Spanish seaman who had been captured by the English returned to Havana to testify that he had seen "signs of horned cattle and a branded mule" at the Chesapeake Bay. The taker of the testimony added: "From these indications I infer that this is where the English had their settlement. I am informed that the natives proved poor friends to the English and that Francis Drake carried off those who survived."

In 1589 Seville received a complete account of the 1585 expedition, taken from testimony by a Spanish captive whom Grenville had kept prisoner for most of his voyage. The account concluded with the opinion that "the people who remained in the settlement should have, by this time, died of hunger, or been exposed to great need and danger." Yet, a subsequent informant said of White's 1590 expedition that his ship had on board "a governour to be left in the settlement they have made in Florida, whither they will go for that purpose."

As late at 1617 a Spanish official who believed that there had been English on Chesapeake Bay for a generation and a half forwarded to the king a deposition by the treasurer of St. Augustine; the deposition included the following comment:

Because the description of the bay of Madre de Dios and of the harbours, with the observations and bearings of their course, is so trustworthy and so necessary for the time when your majesty may be pleased to command that the bay be cleared of the robbers who have occupied and fortified it for thirty years, it seemed well that I should dwell on it at some length.

Philip's reaction to such messages caused a significant change in Spanish policy that was continued by his son and successor, Philip III. Previously the New World's output of precious metals had been used to finance Spain's military-political ventures in Europe. But after Drake's raid, the allocation of funds was altered. Philip II, who previously had been confident that his American sites could be defended by the Spanish fleets located there, sent out an expert on fortifications and an engineer to plan a line of defense against the threat of English attack. The money to erect the tremendous fortresses that extended from San Juan in Puerto Rico and St. Augustine in Florida westward into the Gulf of Mexico (and remain standing at the present time) drained the Spanish royal treasury of funds that could have supported expeditions closer to home. The resulting shortfall was among the important causes of the precipitous decline of the Spanish empire.

In England, after the defeat of the Armada and well within Ralegh's lifetime, the conflict of purposes that had disrupted the Roanoke voyages began to disappear. The wealth of New Spain, fabulous as it was, was seen to be exhaustible. The hope of long-term yields from steady growth began to take precedence over the anticipation of quick riches. By 1597 Francis Bacon was arguing that the

Planting of countries is like planting of woods; for you must make account to leese almost twenty years profit, and expect your recompense in the end. For the principal thing that hath been the destruction of most plantations, hath been the base and hasty drawing of profit in the first years. It is true, speedy profit is not to be neglected, as far as may stand with the good of the plantation, but no further.

In 1613 Michael Lok, a former member of John Dee's scientific circle and son of a London merchant, prefaced his translation of Peter Martyr's *Historie of the West Indies* by commending the Spaniards in the Caribbean for "their constant resolution of Plantation." He thought it

may bee exemplary vnto vs, to performe the like in our Virginea, which being once thoroughly planted and inhabited with our people, may returne a greate benefitte to our Nation in another kinde, as the Indies doe vnto the Spaniard: for although it yeeld not golde, yet is it a fruitfull pleasant countrey, replenished with all good things necessary for the life of man, if they be industrious, who inhabit it.

The life of John Watts, merchant and ship owner of London and captain of White's attempt in 1590 to find the lost colony, further illustrates the change of attitude toward deriving long-term profits by establishing plantations in the New World. When Watts was knighted by James I in 1603, a Spanish observer reported him to be "the greatest pirate that has ever been in this kingdom." That view of Watts was at least partially shared by William Sanderson, the London merchant married to Ralegh's niece, when, on Ralegh's behalf, he made arrangements with Watts to take White to Roanoke. Sanderson prudently placed the indignant captain of the *Hopewell* under heavy bond to proceed directly to Virginia, but the strength of the temptation for Watts to hunt prizes instead is confirmed by White's account of the trip.

Ralegh had just done Watts a good turn. Watts's privateering fleet had been ready to leave for the West Indies when a stay order confined all shipping to port. Ralegh, beseeched by White, secured from the queen an exception that freed the ships *Hopewell, John Evangelist*, and *Little John* and two pinnaces to depart from Plymouth. According to White, it had been agreed

that those 3 ships in consideration of their releasement should take in, & transport a convenient number of passengers, with their furnitures and necessaries to be landed in Virginia. . . . But rather in contempt of the aforesaid order, I was by the owner and Commanders of the ships denied to have any passengers, or any thing els transported in any of the said ships, saving only my self & my chest; no not so much as a boy to attend upon me. . . .

White had not time to appeal to Ralegh in London before Watts's sailing date; once at sea, it soon became evident that the privateer and his associates, "regarding very smally the good of their countreymen in Virginia; determined nothing lesse then to touch at those places, but wholly disposed themselves to seeke after purchase & spoiles. . . ."

Though they sailed on March 20, 1590, it was only after five months of chases and captures that they anchored at Hatteras on August 15—in the prime hurricane season. When they found the word CROATOAN carved on a post at the empty site at Roanoke Island, the obvious thing to do was to go to nearby Croatoan Island, headquarters of Manteo's tribe. But Watts regarded himself as having fulfilled his contract to "touch at those places" and refused to do more. He found his excuse for not searching further in a tropical storm that lashed out of the Caribbean and forced the ships to stand offshore. Unconcerned with the fate of the colony, he did not return to the coast but instead held his eastward course straight on to England.

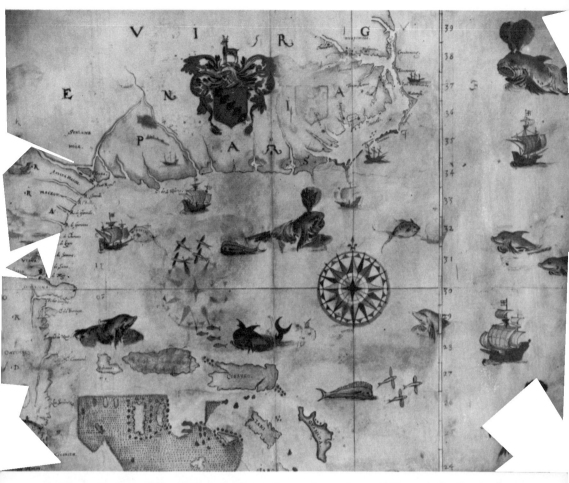

The east coast of North America from the southern shore of Chesapeake Bay to the Gulf of Mexico, with Sir Walter Ralegh's coat of arms near the center. Reproduced from the Page-Holgate facsimiles by permission of the University of North Carolina Press.

Yet, if during most of Elizabeth's reign John Watts was a privateer uninterested in settlements on land, by the turn of the century this sea rover had begun to grasp the potential value of far-flung colonies as entrepots of trade and outposts of empire and had taken a turn toward respectability. He had been elected a London alderman in the 1590s and subsequently achieved knighthood. He was a founder of the East India Company in 1600 and the following year became its governor. In 1606-1607 Sir John Watts was London's lord mayor. In that same year, he entertained King James at his residence near Clothworkers Hall on the occasion of the king's induction as a free brother of that company. In 1609, after a new English venture had been placed at Jamestown on the mid-American coast, he was appointed to his majesty's council for the Virginia Company and joined other adventurers in advancing funds to meet the company's requirements.

Nor was Watts's participation the only overt link between Ralegh's enterprises at Roanoke and the first English colony to survive in America. Richard Hakluyt's interest in western planting was unflagging, from his first association with Ralegh to his death in 1616. Ralegh Gilbert of Compton, son of Sir Humphrey Gilbert and Sir Walter's nephew-namesake, was one of the eight grantees to whom, in 1606, King James awarded the new letters patent for colonization of America under which Jamestown was settled. Sir Thomas Smythe was a member of the group to whom Ralegh made over his interest in the Citie of Ralegh; his son and namesake was later the treasurer of Virginia. And Christopher Newport, commander of the *Little John* during White's voyage of 1590, was captain-general of the fleet of the ships *Susan Constant, Godspeed,* and *Discovery,* which took the now-familiar course south to the Canaries, west to the West Indies, and north to the Virginia coast. At dawn on April 26, 1607, they made their landfall at the southern point of the entrance into Chesapeake Bay.

The *Discourse of the Plantation of the Southern Colonie of Virginia by the English, 1606. Written by that Honorable Gentleman Master George Percy* gives details:

> The six and twentieth day of April, about foure a clocke in the morning, wee descried the Land of Virginia: the same day wee entred into the Bay of Chesupioc directly, without any let or hindrance; there we landed and discouered a little way, but wee could find nothing worth the speaking of, but faire meddowes and goodly tall Trees, with such Fresh-waters running through the woods, as I was almost rauished at the first sight thereof.

So when Christopher Newport and his men rounded the cape that they named for Henry, Prince of Wales, and rowed ashore for their first landing, they touched the site that had been Ralegh's desired destination twenty years before.